Vignettes of a Pianist

Megan Yim

lots of love,

- muy.

Published in Canada for Global Distribution by Golden Brick Road Publishing House Inc. Printed in North America.

ISBN:

Paperback: 9781988736761

Author: meganyim@hotmail.com

Media: hello@gbrph.ca

Book orders: orders@gbrph.ca

Table of Contents

Vignettes of a Pianist

Dedication

This collection of moments both big and small is dedicated to my parents. Though cliché and probably predictable, I just cannot thank them enough, and I can only begin to scrape the visible layer of what they have given me. I say visible because most of a parent's work for their children, I realize, is unseen and oftentimes unspoken. My gratitude for them extends far greater than any feeling I've ever known, and largely because they have given me the gift of music.

Growing up I have always been lucky. I have been blessed and privileged in my environment, and I hold ownership to that. Having music in my life has paved a road for me filled with speed bumps, potholes, collisions, and forks where I have had to choose. Though this road has not always been easy, I have decided to treat them as fortunate moments. The fact that I have the privilege of feeling failure and defeat in the act of learning music is itself a luxury that a great deal of individuals do not have. The one thing I know to be sure, is that it always led me somewhere.

Of course, I have never been on this road alone. To begin, I have to thank my parents for both, literally and figuratively, driving me. All the drives to and from lessons, exams, recitals, competitions, and buying books. All the late night lessons and early morning exams.

I am grateful everyday for the gift of music. I am grateful because I can share it with the rest of the world: with my students, peers, and friends. I know that wherever I am in life, I will always have this gift with me, tucked inside my heart, ready at any moment.

So thank you, mom and dad, for giving me the gift of music. Thank you for paying for every lesson, driving me to every engagement, and sitting at every performance—even when most of them were complete disasters. Thank you for loving me and supporting me unconditionally—even when the road seemed to have ended (but in fact, had just started). Thank you, also, for taking a backseat when you knew to, and not overstepping and helping me decide what to do with my art.

Thank you for letting me follow my dreams.

Mozart's Birthplace, Salzburg, Austria

By: Megan Yim

Vignettes of a Pianist

Dear Reader,

The following is a series of seemingly trivial but defining moments in the life of a pianist. I wrote this because too often in life we glorify our successes—whether it is being on the podium, receiving a diploma, or even a high mark. And while these are admirable and great achievements that deserve a book all on its own, this collection deviates away from those moments. Instead, here, you'll find descriptive scenes that most, if not all, pianists will experience during their studies.

If you've opened this book and you find that you are not a musician or a person in the arts for that matter, I encourage you to still keep reading. I hope that it will bring to light a different angle towards composing a life in the arts, and the poetry that runs through the multifaceted moments that we experience on a daily basis.

The life of a musician is a hard one. But that is not to undermine the life of anyone else. We all have hardships and we all have struggles. This book is a closer look into that of a pianist's. That although we may shine on stage and glisten on video; that although our walls are adorned with large thick sheets of paper, framed, with our names printed in fancy lettering and signed by important people; and that although we are known as "artists" and "magicians" who solve some of the world's toughest issues surrounding mental health. Our lives extend beyond the surface of our polished careers. Our stories have more chapters with footnotes and references than what is on the page. We are filled with complex and unsought experiences. In *Vignettes*, I hope you get a glimpse of these experiences. It is mine to share, and I invite you to view them.

vignette

/vinˈyet/

In literature, a vignette (pronounced vin-yet) is a short scene that captures a single moment or a defining detail about a character, idea, or other element of the story. Vignettes are mostly descriptive; in fact, they often include little or no plot detail. They are not stand-alone literary works, nor are they complete plots or narratives. Instead, vignettes are small parts of a larger work, and can only exist as pieces of a whole story.

Notably, the word vignette comes from the French *vigne* meaning "little vine," and the term specifically arose for the small vines drawn on the pages of printed texts.

So, much like the vines on the page, vignettes are little sections of a much bigger work.[1]

---

[1] https://literaryterms.net/vignette/

I

an unmatched relationship

It is a feeling you get. A desire to learn more, play more, listen more. Black and white keys make the soundtrack of my life; governing my every endeavour, success and downfall. Though there are eighty-eight of them, there are only twelve different truly unique sounds, but represented in different octave intervals. For the pianist's life, we spend our time building a unique relationship with every key: understanding the tone, use, and impact it may have for each respective piece. For me, the keyboard is divided into three parts: bass, middle, and high. The middle is the home base. Here is where we find middle C from the very first lesson. Here is where we take the first steps as a musician and we expand from there.

The bass is owned predominantly by the left hand. On occasion, it will get the spotlight and play a deep, supportive melody. But the majority of the time, the bass is the backbone of the piece. There may be chords, widely broken chordal accompaniment, or a waltz bass line. Though typically undesired, the left hand and bass section is the reason why our music sounds as good as it does. The bass lines give the music a depth of soul, balance from the melody, and a quality that represents a much more authentic and humble vibrance to your music.

The treble is where we can find our melody—usually. Our right hand carries it and we rely too much on this; because although the melody is important and it typically needs to shine above all else, we must remember that the brightest and most "important sounds" do not always lie in what we are conditioned to believe. We must find it within ourselves to hear our own music and the balance that each hand and part offers.

II

the truth

The true pianist never feels like their art is superior. The true pianist does not seek to climb a hierarchy. She, he, or however they choose to identify themselves is always looking for new interpretations. The true pianist searches for context and new ways to share their art. This could be through a blog, Instagram, Facebook, or YouTube. This could be joining a community of other pianists at a local center, or taking lessons not for an exam or competition, but for the sake of learning.

III

the world

As an artist, a musician can only try to scratch the surface of a very rich and ornate universe of classical music. I ask myself, what does being a classically trained musician mean? What are my responsibilities? My duties? Having the privilege and luxury to visit the same locations as such famous composers and musicians of the past, I can only continue to wonder and have an appetite to always learn more. The world of classical music is small, but the universe for which music comes from stretches for distances that in this lifetime I will not be able to comprehend. We can only try. As artists, we should live in fear that we may not be able to learn, share, and hear every musical composition composed by our kind. We should live in fear, not out of shame or lack of confidence, but because we care so much about the world of music that we shed away from our confidence and surrender.

IV

rewarding

At the end of a long day of teaching, I was blessed with a session with my level eight student. She played such beautiful music, and despite my long and tiring day, it is my utmost fortune to be gifted with this incomparable duty that is my job. These minute moments of glory are the pieces of a masterpiece that every artist should cherish.

I was never good enough to be a professional performer. My talents and my lack of virtuosity did not drive me to be in the competitive space of performance, and I'm okay with that. Instead, I found my peace and safe haven in teaching. In teaching, I find the space to create, share, and explore. I am learning not just of education, but of human beings: just how complex, emotional, responsive, and intelligent we are as students young and old.

My favorite part of teaching is sitting on the bench beside my student. I love immersing myself, parallel to the student, where we become one. I love sitting alongside them, investing them in the music and helping them understand the intricacies of this art. I love seeing their faces light up when I teach them something new, and help to comfort them if they feel discouraged. We could be working on a rhythm and there is always an instant of synchronization. We are in sync through the content of what we are working on, but mostly because we are there to pursue the beauty of music. Though they may not know it yet, music will touch their life forever. That idea of them not knowing—that is what is the most pure. Not every student needs to continue with piano studies forever. Their career, relationships, and life do not depend on their commitment to music studies. But so long as they have the privilege of continuing to learn the piano, then the heavier the impact that music will have on them. It will touch them through the way they use their minds, the way they love their friends, and the way they hear a song being played in a grocery store. It will touch them when they learn music theory in high school, the moment they see a piano sitting in the corner of a family friend's living room, and when they feel most confident presenting in front of a crowd.

The power of music is not simply through the shaping of melodies and accuracy of rhythms. The power of music is the unbreakable and invisible ribbon that intertwines with every aspect of daily life. It is the way we learn it and the way we absorb it that helps to weave this ribbon.

V

reflecting

The drive home after an evening full of back-to-back piano lessons is a peaceful one. On tonight's commute home I listened to a new song that I just heard in a mall. Some days I'll listen to a Tchaikovsky concerto. But classical music is not more sacred than any other genre, it is branded as fine art, but what is fine art is probably something I'll never understand . . . such is all the finer things in life. For me, classical music is somewhat acquired. Innately, all music is beautiful. But classical music, for most, is harder to love. There are no words to relate to, multiple harmonies that could overwhelm, and a plethora of options to choose from that you'd never really know which composer to choose, so you just end up listening to Mozart, again. Unless you've performed the piece yourself or listened to it a few times beforehand, a fresh piece of classical music is hard to enjoy in its most organic experience. It is challenging to find the meaning behind its composition, and hold down a convincing story to unfold in our minds.

The sun begins to set and the air is too cool for me to roll down the windows. Traffic is light and my mind is clear. My job is fruitful and rewarding, sometimes frustrating and aggravating, but more often than not it is always fulfilling. I am fulfilled. I pull into my driveway, enter my house, and take a quick washroom break. I know my mom will be sleeping in less than two hours, so I rush down to the black cushioned bench and take a seat. Tonight I will finish my self-assigned practice pieces. I have one more to go from this morning: Chopin's Nocturne in Eb Major op. 9, no. 2. It is a classic, but I don't remember the last time I worked on it until now. I haven't touched this piece in several weeks due to other commitments, but my fingers remember and my mind becomes dependent on them. That's not always good.

Chopin brings a multitude of challenges but one I find difficult to emanate is the tone of a Romantic period. My Petrof is finicky, and as I learn more pieces I find it more and more difficult to adapt and command the keyboard. Just how much pressure, intensity, and care do I need for the sound?

Suddenly, I look to my left and I see six clay figures sitting on my second piano, an upright wooden Baldwin. There sits J.S. Bach, Beethoven, Tchaikovsky, Chopin, Haydn, and Mozart. I'm still missing a few such as Debussy and Schumann, but companies will only make busts of composers that might sell the fastest. It's a society that capitalizes on the idolization of (certain) male (arguably) genius composers. I love them all, I appreciate them all and I am a victim of this idolization society, but I am weak to music and I am weak to art and the truth is, I'll take anything art can give me because I only have myself to give back.

So I'm done with Chopin for the night. I move on to some new music my teacher has given me. Some Schubert. Growing up I was told that Schubert was too "hard" for me, and that there's no point in tackling it, and that I was much better off with Mozart to suit my much more "playful" and "youthful" style. The opening of Schubert's A Major Sonata D. 664 is glorious, romantic. Lyrical, and extremely satisfactory to my ears and heart. Music is my savior.

VI

balance

The opening of Haydn's last Eb Major sonata features a French overture. Producing a full, rich, yet also innocent tone in the opening four chords is a challenge. She sat at the piano for over twenty minutes repeating those chords over and over again until she heard success. The balance of all four pitches both in the right and left hand is endlessly difficult because every time she touches the keyboard there is a slight difference in strength and intention. The most challenging of all—is once the pianist discovers the balance, she must duplicate that balance, which in reality, feels impossible at times. But not all the time.

VII

failure

As a pianist you will come to know failure as much or even more than you will know success. As with any artist, you will face rejection and setbacks in the most cruel, subjective, confusing, and not to say the least, the most contradicting of ways. The trick, here, is to realize that all these denied opportunities are not meant to set you back any more than they are to push you forward. The term "setback" is confusing because while failures are meant to be denied attempts at success, much of popular culture promotes failure as catalysts of success and stepping stones to a brighter opening.

The important question to ask then, is just how do we deal with failure and rejection after it happens again and again? Will we ever run out of resilience? Will we reach a breaking point and give up? I think I've learned over the years that if you love something or someone enough, you must fight for it and defend it. There goes a saying that we must not push too hard because if something is meant to happen then it will. But what happens when something appears too unlikely, yet we are pushed down from it time and time again?

I love the piano and I love what I do when I teach, so I am determined to spend the rest of my life fighting for it. If you are an artist you will agree that your art is one of— if not the most—sacred aspects of your life. Your art must be preserved within yourself before you share it with others.

Failures are not representations of your competence, talent, and most of all, love for your art. Failure is simply a direction you're pushed toward, from which you should continue to seek further contentment and fulfilment with your art. Embrace all sides of it.

VIII

disruptions

On the black bench in your living room, you return to the same set of black and white keys that you've turned your attention to for the last twenty years. They've never changed. Maybe a few keys have yellowed a bit and some of the notes have gone out of tune due to overplaying and lack of regular tuning. But the shell and its strings are intact and you've returned to it because it's the only safe space in your life right now. You look around you and you see music sprawled out across the side of the instrument, on the floor beside the yellow chair, and a few copies peeking out from last year's recital. Then the real, heartbreaking, truth pulling question hits you: Just how long do I have to learn all this music before society's expectations disrupt my course of passion chasing?

The truth I've realized and concluded as a pianist in all my life is that life and society will charge forward with no end, to try and interrupt your journey. They will challenge your strength to hold on, pull on your legs so you must go slower, and steal away feelings of joy and love that you once held dear to your heart.

Disruptions include: pressure to choose a more "stable" route for career and education, long term relationships questioning your level of commitment to your partner versus your art, and the ever pressing "business" and "corporate" side of fulfilling your duty as a musician in the industry as opposed to following your natural inclination to learn music to, well, learn music.

So just how do we conquer and fight these disruptions? I feel that they are inevitable and, for the most part, even necessary. As humans, and especially, as artists, we do not progress and learn until we've been challenged by the worst of the enemies, and life itself, I think, is art's biggest enemy. One of my very first English professors at university once told our class, "The best part about art is that it does absolutely nothing. It is useless and expects nothing from us. Art hurts, art feels, and it does all of that so we, as the readers, listeners and observers, do not have to. That is the beauty of art."

Vignettes of a Pianist

IX

teaching

So what, then, would be the point of playing the piano? For if art is useless and life would give us endless disruptions in chasing our dreams; what, then, would be the purpose we set on pursuing piano performance?

I dare not speak for others and I dare not advise others, despite what this book appears to be. For me, it is the honor and privilege to be the pedagogue of my art, and to share and experience my art with others. This is through the practice of teaching and guiding others. Teaching has been, for me, and I'm sure for most other teachers out there, the single most rewarding practices I have done in my entire life thus far. Setting aside all egotistical notions of being "better" and "superior" to the student, but let us merely focus on the energy of being with another individual who seeks to learn, and know, and share your art with you in the same space—that, itself, is beauty.

I rarely get the opportunity to take a step back and analyze the space of my classroom. But when I do, I am always careful to seek out the positive energy that I seek to cultivate. Am I always successful? Probably not. Teaching is hard. It is challenging and gruelling, and may be very frustrating at times. But to counteract all of those—there are the rare but miraculous moments of reward; and that, is why I teach.

The art of teaching is no forte of mine, nor do I claim to be honorable enough to offer advice on it. I can only offer my truest experience of what I've lived and observed in my past. Every child and student is so different in their upbringing and personality that I myself feel humbled and ironed out every day that I am a teacher. Their household environment, parental discipline style, and general interests and behaviors vary so much that I feel the world has opened up to an infinite amount of combinations that no one could ever prepare for.

X

artists

So it is, the realization that you are a smidge of musical offering in this world of starving, ambitious, and maybe even angry artists. In times of rejection you realize that your work and what you've trained is incomparable to an infinite amount of individuals beyond your reach that want the exact same thing as you: to do what they love, and get paid for it. Money is the only way to the basic necessities of survival and well, if we can get that money through the means of our very existing passions in life, then that would be undeniably ideal.

The trouble is, just how does an artist go about not starving and succumb to the pressure of achieving this ideal?

Considering the fact that every "starving artist" is objectively talented, we have to narrow it down to a few very important possibilities:

- You are born fortunate. Such as I. When you are born fortunate you have the tools and resources already there to support your dreams and stand by you as you trip and fall again and again (both on a physical level and musically technical level). I have loving parents, a finely tuned piano, and enough financial support for lessons, master classes, recitals, competitions, books . . . the list goes on.

- You just get very lucky. We all know how luck works – being at the right place at the right time, saying the words that others cannot think of fast enough . . . it's no secret. Being lucky is one of the most sought after qualities that nobody knows how to work for. There is no degree you can chase to be lucky nor is there a certain kind of person it takes to be lucky. All there is, I suppose, is karma. If you put out good in the world, you will receive at least a little bit of that back.

So I think being fortunate and being lucky are just factors of living the life of an artist. Some are more fortunate and some have more luck. To combat these forces I think takes great determination and courage because you will be defeated more than once in your life, and you will be knocked down for more performances than you might imagine.

The "vignette" here, I suppose, is the tableau of the silent artist. The one who does not speak out but sits quietly in her room practicing all day long—running through each Hanon exercise like having to brush her own teeth, trying out that D minor chord. One could argue that there is no such thing as a silent pianist because in order to become a pianist one must create music. But pianists do not speak while they play—some may sing—but hardly can they carry out a full conversation while working on their art. This goes for every individual who studies any craft, for that matter. But the beauty of creating music "silently" is often overlooked. The music speaks for the artist and often times it is the perfect and only way for the artist to represent herself.

XI

edifice

We are often reminded not to focus too much on the tangible items in life and focus on the immeasurable aspects such as love and curiosity. We are told that it is not where you went or what you ate, but who you were with and how you felt. While I believe this and have experienced and recollected on these very instances myself—where I've had to tell myself to detach the physical from the immeasurable, I do beg to differ on some cases.

I was at Leonard Gilbert's Chopin benefit concert one Saturday night, which was held in a hall that I lived so many memories in. It is a hall not too large, but still so grand that the size of it is but of a minute detail to me. The hall seats a maximum of 120 listeners, but on stage looking out, it could easily seem like five hundred. The seats, though this was not always the case, are relatively comfortable to the point where an audience member probably wouldn't mind sitting for over an hour. The stage itself is extremely well lit to a point where you, as the performer, would feel your face burning up like the sun and wish for nothing but to be *on* the sun rather than performing. The stage is paved with hardwood flooring, so the heel of your shoes always hit the surface with the right amount of "tap" that is just the perfect balance between not too awkward of a silence and borderline annoying. On it, sits a majestic Steinway & Sons grand, the kind of piano that most students and even some professional musicians could ever dream of playing. When the lid is lifted up, the sound bounces from every corner of the room and lands right in your own ear. The Steinway, like all Steinways, has the power to make your own mistakes sound beautiful and the flawless performances to the same degree of the melodies played by angels in the heavens. All along the facing walls of the hall are paintings of various iconic composers of the Western hemisphere. Those of J.S. Bach, Beethoven, Brahms, and Liszt adorn the room. One would even wonder whether there existed composers outside of the euro-centric world of music. Why, of course there are. Maybe one day we'll see a Canadian composer hung on the wall or even a woman composer. But that's for another book.

The room holds an immensely sacred place in my heart as it represents my beginnings and continuity of my staggering artistic career. That hall has seen my first piano recital, competition, various lessons, and final performance exams. The memories of me walking up to the stage are as vivid as my recollection of what I did just this morning. The mental image of me completely blanking out on stage and looking down at the keys are so clear that I can still hear the way my heart thudded inside me, while I feared that the audience would hear it just as loudly.

The hall is, now, even home to my students' performances and plays a vital role in their development as musicians. It is the perfect space for my students and I consider it a rare privilege to be able to share this space with them. Through this space, not only have I created music, but I've also shared it too. Through this space, I've introduced a physical common ground between me and my students, allowing them into a world that touches me so deeply they don't even know.

So, as I was sitting listening to the intense virtuosic demands of Gilbert's rendition of Chopin's Ballade no. 3 in A-flat, I looked up and had a flashback of the previously purple tinted hall. A few years back the hall underwent an upgrade in renovations, which could be seen as a strip of my childhood; but I view it as the parallel maturity of my own life. Like most stages of maturity— the hall now takes on a much more crisp and professional look, giving the feeling of seriousness and respectability. The ways in which I've grown into my own personhood and how the hall has done the same. So I believe that tangible items such as buildings and performance halls are important to musicians because they give us the space to perform and create. The defining moments of the hall and where I sat and what light shone on me as I performed are part of who I am. In fact, it is all I am.

XII

the fight

What it must be like for children who are in multiple extracurricular sessions a week; and amidst all the chaos of swimming, and soccer, and math tutor, how does piano take a role? The question we may have, as pianists, is ask to what right do we have to deem piano as a superior art or craft than to learning how to swim or play hockey? I suppose we cannot. Learning art and playing the piano has always, and will always be viewed as, "secondary" in terms of what really matters in life—Math, Science, English, French, etc. Music is not as "important" or "necessary," only an "outlet for expression." Only.

It is not a competition, but it is a severe challenge for a piano teacher to have to "fight" their way in for their student to understand that practicing the piano should be a vital part of everyday routine. My hopes, as a piano teacher, is that my students find the classroom and thirty minute lesson window as a safe space for creation and cultivation. But this space may be produced only with the collaboration between the student and parent, to which the values of practice are cherished.

I stare at the student as he tells me on a late Tuesday afternoon how busy he was that week from soccer practice, to swim meets, to art class, to karate. He looks at me with a genuine reaction because he truly is not lying. These are actual items on his agenda and even though he feels the need to list out everything, what he truly means to say is, "I just didn't have time to practice."

As he finishes, I continue to stare at the student even though he has finished speaking. What am I to do? Tell him to quit his other activities? Even if it were his decision, it would not be that simple. So, in the two seconds of silence, of me trying to figure out what to say next, we sit there and dwell on an endless time frame of possibilities. The endlessness that would bring a universe where everyone could have time for everything. Where piano, soccer, and karate were not competitors in a fight, but rather teammates that coexisted, and each student felt comfortable and at ease with balancing every subject. The endlessness where not only would there be enough time to practice and attend every lesson wholeheartedly with their fully undivided attention, but where there would be time to foster that love and passion that comes along with every kind of art and sport. The time that it takes for an art to cultivate is much more demanding than many assume. And while there are individuals out there who have been fortunate enough to recognize such a passion, for piano, for instance, there are also millions more who are simply less fortunate and have not been able to come to that conclusion. They have been provided with far too many choices and opportunities in life. The abundance of choice and opportunity which may have harmed them more than anything else, I suspect. It is because with this abundance comes the difficult task of achieving balance in character; the idea that for a child to grow up well-rounded is to expose them to multiple different subjects in the arts, sports, and sciences. While I agree with this notion completely and think that every child should be as well rounded as possible, the idea of being well-rounded and balanced distorts and does not agree with the idea of being passionate. Students are suffocating in the midst of opportunity and as teachers, we sit in their suffocation too. My job, then, as a teacher is to help these students breathe. The oxygen mask, which introduces the breeding ground for cultivating an appreciation for the arts. The offering that we can give to our students that they are doing great.

Any student who walks into my classroom is fortunate. They have parents who have allocated money to pay not only for these lessons, but the books, additional materials, and even the gas needed to drive them here. Even if your teacher goes to your house, you've adjusted your entire schedule to fit this thirty minute time slot in.

Parents work excruciatingly hard to put their children in the best of situations. They have the world's most challenging job. Part of this job, sometimes, is to put their child in the fight to be the best of themselves. I can only express gratitude to have the opportunity to share my music with their children.

XIII

the lost artist

There is such a kind of person called the "lost artist" that I feel outnumbers the found and existing artists of our world. The lost artist started as the child who, from their early ages of between five to eight years were enrolled in music lessons beyond their will (at some odd times maybe at their request), and then encouraged to pursue the following eight to ten practical levels. This is most common within piano students, as the piano is one of the most accessible "home" instruments and parents hold the piano as a highly esteemed skill which, in turn, promotes self-learning, confidence, cognitive awareness, creativity, and so forth.

Yet, despite the benefits and despite the parents' financial and emotional support for

their child's musical "career", the lost artist, indeed, loses his or her way due to the
more "important" priorities in life. That is—
studying hard to get good marks, get accept-
ed into an elite post-secondary institution,
land a stable job, and, you know, just "suc-
ceed" in any other way that would still be
better than that of a life of the pianist. In
turn, these artists become, well, lost. They
themselves are not lost, they are clearly very
intelligent and hardworking individuals
who will no doubt climb their way upward
amongst the corporate heroes and entrepre-
neurial titans of commercial society.

Instead, it is the world that loses them. It
is every human and living entity that will
never bear witness to their art ever again.
The potential and possibility of the rest of us
being graced and honored by their music—
vanished. We are then, left, with the rare
gems of artists that continue to pursue their
craft and bless us with the greatest movie
soundtracks, indie albums, commercial
jingles, and telemarketer "hold" music that
human history would ever live to hear. To
the rest, they are lost to us.

It is with a heavy heart that we should mourn for these lost artists because although they may be happy, fulfilled, and successful; what they may or may not know is that their art will forever be lost to us. Perhaps if they continued to play they would become the greatest pedagogues, inspirational performers, or legendary composers of our time. Perhaps if they had supporters and teachers who believed more in their art we would have a different set of names on the list of Grammy nominees, the Hollywood Walk of Fame, or more composer biographies on the bookshelf.

Thus, we must not forget about them. These lost artists. Though we may not know them. Though we may never hear their music. Though we may never even know how many there are of them. We must remember that they are everywhere around us. They may be the CEO of your favorite coffee shop. They may be the engineer that invented your smartphone. They may be your Uber driver. We will never know. What we do know though, and what we can be certain about, is that the music we listen to on our daily commute, the theme song to your favorite show, or the jingle to the newest soda commercial–the world is not limited to only a few names of composers we know. There are a lot of artists out there. Some of them found, but most of them lost.

XIV

the drive (one)

"Let's go." Fear. Shudder. Regret. The sound of the car starting, there's a blizzard coming, but it doesn't matter. Put on your jacket. What books do you need for today? You forgot to photocopy the fourth page, again. Maybe if you "forget" your Czerny you won't have to play it. But she might have an extra copy.

"Hurry up." What would be the harm in being late? Wouldn't that mean a shorter lesson? No. She would just extend it. You probably should have practiced after school today. And yesterday. And the day before. How does a week pass by so fast? There's a knot in your stomach now because you had to rush through dinner.

"Ready?" The slam of the car door is like the inauguration of a weekly ceremony that you never want to attend. When are you ever ready? When would you ever be? Let's just get this over with. One hour, right?

What is actually a fifteen minute car ride always feels like five. You could never arrive there slow enough. On the drive there, you hear your mom's thoughts shouting at you. Shouting at you that you should have practiced more this week and why were you on YouTube instead of reviewing your scales? You hear it all and you shiver. You look out the window and the sun is starting to set. It was supposed to be beautiful, but somehow this drive made everything appear less than. It's like the notion of simply going to the lesson extracted every ounce of beauty out of the world. What good were sunsets if you couldn't appreciate them? What good was the luxury of your mom driving you if you hated where you were going?

The car turns into the parking lot and your fingers fumble to undo the seatbelt. Like clockwork. Every Tuesday at 7:55pm, your mom's car makes that final turn and as the building where you'll be spending the next sixty-five minutes comes into view, your fingers know what to do.

"See you in an hour."

XV

the drive (two)

"Let's go." The sound of the car starting, there's a blizzard coming, but it doesn't matter. Put on your jacket. What books do you need for today? You forgot to photocopy the fourth page, again. Let's bring the Czerny in case you have to review those 16th note arpeggios again. Let's grab the Schumann too, just in case.

"Ready?" The slam of the car door is the inauguration of a weekly ceremony that you're honored to attend. Of course you're ready. It's Tuesday. It's the one day of the week featuring the escape you needed. The day of the week where mistakes are expected and nothing else matters except what you create.

The commute is always a relaxing one. You look out the window and there's your old high school and that tree that's grown taller than you ever imagined to see. There's the house you used to spend Saturdays at, but you don't go there anymore because you no longer talk to that person. You wonder where she is now. You flip open to the front page of the Beethoven Sonatas because you're bored. Don't you just love thematic tables of content? You try your hardest to sight sing in your head one of the ones you've never played before. You can't sight sing.

"I'll come back to pick you up." The car turns in and you see the light on inside the room. Her silhouette roams from the piano to a larger table, probably with a four hour old coffee. 7:52pm. The lesson starts in 8 minutes, but you always like to sit there early anyways. A full eight minutes of silence waiting for the door to open to your lesson. A full eight minutes where you're not expected to be anywhere else but there, in the chair, waiting for the hour to begin.

"There she is!" That's how she always welcomed me. Not, "Come on in" or "Hi!" It was a signifier of my attendance—that in fact, yes, you arrived and you are here. There you are. 8:00, on the dot. You wait as the other student gathers her books to exchange places with you. Her—because for the last seven years it was always the same student who had the lesson before you. It was always her, but you would never learn her name, never know which was her favorite piece, or whether she even liked to play piano at all. She would always be known as "the student before me" and that was it. She doesn't smile, she never does though. Maybe she's just one of those people who just never smiles, even if she really likes something. The problem is you'll just never know. She zips up her jacket to leave and finally gives you a warm smile— could be a smile of relief that "YES! I'm out of here," or that she's just trying to be courteous. Probably the former.

Here I am. In front of the keys again. You open your roughed up Beethoven volume and feel the wear on page fifty-four, where the first movement starts. 8:01.

XVI

the drive (three)

"It's the third time this has played on the station today." 2007 Fergie's "Big Girls Don't Cry" was the anthem to me and my mom's summer. Every Saturday we'd go grocery shopping and we'd wait until this song came on throughout 9:00 to 11:00am. That summer it frequented 99.9FM's mix at least once an hour. That was a good year for pop music. I know it was a good year because I remember it. Unforgettable is the word I think. The third time "Big Girls" played on the radio that day was during the drive to my piano lesson. The lesson started at 11:45am. Listening to twenty-first century music in the twenty-first century is almost ridiculous to think about—because when else would you listen to it?

Music, like any art, reflects culture and society. We listen to what makes us feel good and dance to what moves us most. But when you learn an instrument and take up lessons, the music you learn and the exercises you're told to work on are not at all reflections of current socio-cultural standpoints. If a student, eight years old, takes up piano in 2007, she does not learn "Big Girls Don't Cry" in the fifth week. Instead, the music classroom turns into somewhat of a time machine, where traveling back in time to the greats of Bach, Mozart, and Beethoven are nothing short of mandatory. Still, now, no one has questioned this kind of time traveling, and no one seems to complain about it. Except the students themselves.

So the order goes like this: "Hot Cross Buns," "Mary Had a Little Lamb," Minuet in G major, a Gavotte if your teacher feels like it, and then Clementi's Sonatina in C Major op. 36 no.1. Yeah, you know the one. So I have students ask me all the time why they must learn music composed so long ago. Actually, no, they never actually ask. But I know they want to. So I answer their question without even asking. I explain the significance of legacy and the urgency of art. I explain what it means to be a musician through and through. I explain that my mission is to share the music of some of the greatest found artists and to take full responsibility to fulfill our purpose as true artists.

Within the walls of a music classroom, we defy the laws of physics and time travel. We open scores from the past and play music from past centuries.

Time travelling with music is sacred. It is sacred because unlike the Fergies, and Lady Gagas, and Jonas Brothers of our time, we can't just walk into a Starbucks and ask the barista to play it and have them give you a quick nod. We can't just request it at our high school winter formal without your friends questioning your taste. We can't just mention it to your aunt on Saturday night at family dinner. We simply just can't do that. So we must resort to our time that we exist in solitude within the four walls of practicing and taking lessons.

XVII

the drive home (four)

"How was it?" She does not turn toward you, but looks down at the gear and shifts it into reverse to back out of the parking spot where she was waiting for you. Your mom was waiting for an answer. Trouble is, there is never an answer to this question because you could not possibly explain how it truly went. On your end, it was pretty bad. You didn't practice all week and you barely absorbed what you worked on. You brought all four books, but you only worked on one of the pieces. You played a few scales, none of them accurate, and messed up on identifying all the intervals. For the last sixty minutes, all you could think about was the science report you have to hand in first thing tomorrow morning.

You buckle the seatbelt and feel the warmth of the car heater hit your hands. Normally you'd be grateful for this heat in the winter air, but you've had the last hour to warm up your hands that the last thing you need right now is more heat.

"Good." This was the answer you gave her every week. This was the answer you gave every week because there is no other answer that would be considered quite as acceptable. What are you supposed to do? Give a full break down of every bar you worked on? The fact that you should have reviewed your scales before you left the house earlier tonight? The fact that you didn't even want to come to the lesson tonight because you have the weight of school work on your shoulders, and your crush isn't going to the school dance on Friday, and so you've lost all chances of slow dancing with him, again?

No, you can't tell her any of this.

The car turns out of the parking lot and you look over to your mom, wondering what she did in the last hour. You live too far away for her to go home, and there's not enough time in an hour to do anything productive like go grocery shopping or the bank. The only ideas that might be plausible is her getting a coffee at the Tim Hortons next to the music school.

As the car drives down a dimly lit street, your mind wanders to an image of your mom, sitting at Tim Hortons. Alone. The lid is off because she's not going anywhere that would require her to have a to-go cup. The heat of the supposedly fresh and still steaming hot coffee rises up from the cup and fogs her glasses. She looks down at her watch, 8:09pm. Still fifty-one minutes to go before she has to come back to pick me up. This was the age before smartphones and tablets and not every Tim's had Wi-Fi yet.

When we think about gratitude for our parents, we often remember the big things. We remember the tuition they paid for or the car they bought us. We thank them for changing our diapers or cooking us dinner every day. While these things are worth every ounce of our gratitude, we should also remember the much smaller details of their efforts. Sitting there, alone, waiting for your lesson to finish when instead she could be at home on the couch watching TV.

Sitting there, alone, looking at her watch every ten minutes when she could be spending more quality time with the rest of your family.

Sometimes, it is not simply based on what they give us or what they sacrifice for us. Sometimes, it is about what they decide for us. By choosing to drive me to piano lessons and choosing to stay at the coffee shop next door, it would make sure she's on time to pick me up after the lesson. If she's on time, I could get home faster and therefore get to do my school work even faster. It's all in the equation.

And though I'll never truly know what my mom did while I was at piano lessons, it made me realize that I should appreciate the lessons even more. I should appreciate the lessons not because it costs money, not only because I was blessed to even have lessons in the first place, but I should appreciate it because my mom appreciates it for me. She decided it for me. And just by attending the lesson? Well, that was the least I could do.

So the car turns into your driveway and she lets you out first before parking in the garage. You get in the door, leave the piano books on the bench, and run upstairs to turn on your laptop and finish up the math homework before the science report. 9:12pm. It's not that late, but you know that Tuesdays are always like this. Piano lesson nights always lead you to working late nights. But that's okay. What is important is that your mom is home now, too, and she gets to relax on the couch, watching TV, and spend time with your father downstairs.

XVIII

the drive home (five)

8:59pm. "Already?" She asks. You nod silently because you, too, are saddened that the hour has come to a close. You quickly gather your books together and wave her goodbye because you know that there will be a next week, a next week, a week after that, and the week after that.

"How was it?" You get into the car with the edges of your mouth curved up. The only hour of the week that gives you true freedom and inspiration. The hour that allows you to step into your creative space, apart from all the traffic and congestion that is your life. Of course it was good. It has been good for the past year now. You look down at your music and then back up at the digital clock: 9:02pm. If you get home by 9:13pm, you could scarf down dinner by 9:25pm, and play again at 9:30pm. You need to do this as soon as possible because by ten o'clock your mom would be asleep. Then at ten, you could spend the next two and a half hours finishing up your homework for the evening.

The car pulls out of the parking lot and you watch as the orange tinted street lights brighten up the dark and winding road. The road is technically a bridge over the highway and you look to your right to see a few cars streaming up and down—the cars of late-night workers just finishing up their shift, or just about to start it. Maybe the cars with parents driving their kids home from piano lessons, too.

The thing is, you took it for granted. What would seem like an eternal weekly schedule of routine piano lessons would actually be cut short just shy of two decades. Nothing lasts forever. You would leave each lesson unchanged and without a worry because you'd just go back next week and improve anyway. But until when would next week be the last week?

Years pass. Summers are filled with vacations here and there, and Christmases are always meant for family time. Exam times are always stressful, and competition season never quite seems to come at a reasonable pace. For almost twenty years, you practiced (or tried to) six days a week, and by the seventh, it was time for the lesson again.

The drive home from piano lesson was always like leaving a special place that you never knew was special. It was like that one restaurant your family went to every Saturday until it closed down; or the one elementary school teacher that you had fifteen years ago and finally retired; or the one friend who lived down the street from you since you were ten gets married and moves away. Piano lessons were special places because they were safe. Yes, they did not always go well. Yes, your teacher was not always proud or happy with you. But while you might have been criticized or discouraged for not practicing or playing the notes correctly—just remember that that critique and discouragement does not leave the room. Just like your favorite dish at your family's favorite restaurant, the same jokes your elementary teacher used to tell, or the good times you'll always have with your next-door friend.

We forget that the moments that build us up are sometimes contained in special places in our lives. Piano lessons existed not only to teach you piano, but because they played a vital role in placemaking. The act of creating significant landmarks of where we were in life and what we could depend on. It was the idea that the moment you walked into the room, there stood the piano at the back, your teacher's canvas tote bag overflowing with sheet music lopped over the black fold-up chair in the corner. Your teacher staring at you, welcoming you with a happy smile even though things ended poorly the week before. Then you'd sit down in front of the piano, and you would open up the books that you brought from home, and (supposedly) practiced for the last six days. You'd play for her, and though her feedback was not always positive, at least you could see it coming.

We forget, I think, that special places need not always be happy places. Just like how your favorite restaurant may not always have the best service, or that you may have done poorly on a test with your school teacher, or had a fight with your best friend. Special places don't even promise happiness or a happy ending, for that matter, but they do promise safety. And they serve as a reminder that we are more than who we are as individuals, but we are how we interact with the rest of the world.

The car turns into your driveway and your mom lets you out first, so you can get into the house quickly. You slam the car door shut and run inside. You look down at your music, then smell the food from the kitchen that your dad left for you just an hour ago. Before walking over to reheat your food, you sit down, open your book that you had just played twenty minutes ago, and practice, again. Your fingers float on the keyboard to remind you, not of the same piece that you practiced over and over again before, but that it brings you back. Back to that special place that would one day retire.

XIX

the bench

Does it go clockwise or counter clockwise? The heads of the audience look like darkened clouds that would only settle from the storms of the keyboard. It's clockwise. A cough echoes ...

The fidgeting between turning the bench knobs clockwise or counter, going up or down, mixed with the expectant stares you cannot see. The buzz of the warm light that's already inducing a sweaty glow you didn't ask for. You're red. You didn't always feel this way, but as you get older, your nerves seem to take over your body, causing you to shake from head to toe. It's as if your entire body suddenly morphed into a bow attempting *vibrato* on an invisible violin.

Last night I felt like the persona of an artist—the keyboard was my palette and the music was my masterpiece. But the music and the musician is one. I became the music and I was beside myself as a human who walked the Earth. Every note that sounded, every chord rung, and every harmony shared—a part of me had surrendered to my art. A professor I once had, said that the best part about art is that it asks absolutely nothing of us. But even though it doesn't demand anything from us—the door is always open. You walk through it and if you want, you may give as much or as little of it as you wish. The peculiar realization is that I don't feel as though I've truly surrendered until now. There is a reason why a performer is tired after a performance—it is because a part of themselves has been given away, and their heart has truly felt the music. The tone, what the tone produces achieves this. So in the end, the goal is to attempt to convey to the audience what you are feeling too. Just what do you want your audience to feel? Is it the yearning for love? The devastation of a divided country? The endless dissatisfaction of life? When you release music—it is not measured by the quality of the performance in terms of accuracy or timing, but more on your willingness to share your music with the world, and when you do that, the world becomes a better place.

When you've finished, the audience claps, as is necessary. As are the rules of spectatorship, audience participation, and respect. When the audience shows support, you're meant to feel celebrated, proud even. Sometimes, though, there's a long moment of loneliness. When you place your hand on the ledge of the piano to take a bow to show a sign of gratitude. In those two seconds, who shares that gratitude with you? Who is sharing the victory with you? Is it the audience? No, they're the ones who instigate the victory.

Musicians celebrate alone, and that's no one's fault or flaw, it is just the nature of being an artist. We must be strong enough to celebrate our successes alone, just as strong as we are when we celebrate our failures. You try to make out your mom and dad and you see the lines of their faces, but it's not completely clear. Nevermind that, the important thing is that you know they're there. In that moment of bowing and loneliness there plays a silent reel of memory. In this reel you will see the times you didn't want to practice. The times you didn't want to go to lessons. The times you couldn't figure out the correct fingering. That's because you won't remember the successful sixteenth-note passages or the challenging left-hand arpeggiated pattern. You won't remember it because when you celebrate alone. The easiest thing to do is remember the hardships.

XX

the visit

You ring the doorbell, and you and your parents are welcomed in. There it is, in the corner. The black, shiny instrument standing on its four short legs pinned against the wall like a magnetic boulder. The lid is shut because whomever the instrument was purchased for hadn't touched it in years. Now, a table runner made of lace (resembling a doily) runs along the top of the cover. Sitting atop the runner are four picture frames. Yes, holding pictures of the person for whom the piano was purchased.

The piano stares back at you because it knows what's coming next. You walk in, take your shoes off, and you and your family are offered a drink. Usually juice or water, but you've been taught to decline the first offer.

You take a seat in a spot on the couch away from where the "adults" will be conversing, and angle yourself purposely away from the peripheral view of the instrument. Maybe if they can't see you seeing it, they won't ask.

"Play for us!" Oh, they asked. They always ask. They think it's a way of showing appreciation for you. They want you to believe that they actually want you to play. But you had played this morning and the morning before that, so why on earth would you want to play right now in a foreign space in front of a foreign piano?

But you have to, of course. Denying the request would only add further guilt after. Denying the request would only mean that you've wasted your mom's lesson money and that you don't value her efforts for putting you in lessons at all. You set down the mug full of tea that's now close to cold, and your brain runs in circles as it tries to recall the piece you're about to show them. Which one should I choose? That boring Bach *gigue*? No . . . you barely remember the left hand for that one. 2nd Movement Sonata?

Too slow, they won't find it impressive, even though it's the hardest of them all. Your favourite and best one is the Czerny *etude*, but that is the farthest away from "musical" to the untrained ear. You walk over to the black bench and open the lid to reveal the keyboard. It's a Yamaha because that's what most families get their children at the beginning. Affordable, reliable, and sufficient quality. You settle for the Bach gigue because that's the most "impressive" you have thus far, and at least if you miss a few notes in the left hand, the right hand rhythm will still carry you through.

You finish the piece and the sparse applause brings you a feeling of pride and confidence. It wasn't so bad after all and you wish you could play again. But after one piece they've had enough. You've proven yourself worthy. You've made good use of your mom's money, effort, and time. Now you want to go home and practice and work on the left hand, so you'd be better prepared for next time.

Conversations move on and the topic of the piano subsides. In a world where taking piano is just one chess piece of the extracurricular agenda, there needs to be nothing more than a one-time demonstration of what you've learned. There is no interest in what you want to do with it afterwards because surely anything in the arts would be absurd.

So we pedal on, literally and figuratively, as we are subtly discouraged from any form of passion beginning to flame.

XXI

practicing

Page 133 ... oh it's 233. The week slipped by, and it's the day before the lesson and you finally mustered up the energy to attempt a practice session. Your life is piled with tests and projects, and crushes, and school dances. Your parents think you're not going anywhere in life and your teacher is ready to drop you. It's the dead of winter and your hands are so frozen you can barely feel the key as your reach for an octave. When was the last time you practiced this piece? Probably two weeks ago ...

You didn't show this piece to her last lesson, so she's probably going to want to work on it this week. Thing is, she's not going to be impressed. It was supposed to be memorized by this week; trills, resolutions, phrasing and all. You were supposed to perfect bar thirty-five with the right-hand ornaments, and fix the cross rhythms on the last page. Of course you didn't because you kept putting it off and here we are. Once again, feeling defeated.

The thing about defeat is that there should always be a winner. Who wins, though? We feel defeat because for every day we do not practice what actually happens is the loss of the skill.

For every moment you put-off practicing, your fingers lose their touch and your mind loses interest.

Page 233. Starting from the beginning, but you hit the first sixteenth-note passage and you've already tripped over your fingers. Your fingers forgot how to move. You know you should practice slowly, but what is the fun in that? You do not yet know that hard work and proper results are not always achieved with speed. You do not yet know just how important the virtue of patience is.

The virtue of patience in learning the piano extends beyond the bench. It extends beyond perfecting the trill and completing a chordal passage. It even extends beyond completing the actual piece itself, sometimes up to twenty-four pages in length.

XXII

erasers

Eraser crumbs fall on the score's ledge like raindrops on a sad rainy Sunday. You've written in the wrong fingering and now the page looks messy. You were supposed to make these changes three weeks ago, but you couldn't muster up the energy and motivation to actually pick up a pencil to rewrite them. Now there's eraser debris sitting at the bottom of your music. Messy.

No one will clean up those crumbs unless you do. Piled together, lined up along the crevices of the ledge that keep your music upright. When the crumb falls, it is by chance which crevice it chooses, bundled up eraser bits that hold the pencil markings you no longer wanted. If we were to unfurl those eraser crumbs and microscopically reveal what each of them holds, revealing the truths about mastering a piece of music. The amount of lead required for every finger number, phrase marking, crescendo, pedalling . . . the list goes on. And when we know how it's done; when we see that we've got it right, we take it away. We erase it and let the remnants of those corrections and additions fall from the page. Vanished, so that any trace, evidence, and sign that can point to your flaws and imperfections is, in fact, irretraceable, lost, and in the process of being forgotten.

On exam day, you hand in the freshly cleaned score. The piece is masterfully played; not because you know what's on the page, but because of the pencil markings. You know what's on the page because your teacher had picked up the HB and wrote in three, two, three, two, one, two, one on the trill in the third measure. You know what's on the page because the chordal progression was so complex you needed extra guidance on where to change the pedal. You know what's on the page, and you've successfully memorized it because where you'll play a crescendo in the arpeggiated episode from measure sixty-four, there in fact is no crescendo written at all. There in fact is no printed version of the fingering on top of the trill, and there is nothing but "con pedale" at the opening of the piece.

There is nothing but black ink on the page, and everything you know, and everything you've memorized and come to know, has been completely erased. The only evidence is in two places: your performance and the eraser crumbs lying on the crevices atop the piano's ledge.

And so, since we cannot bottle up our eraser debris without society thinking of us as ridiculous; we must stand for them in performance. We must diligently play for our music but ultimately, the playing and the performance itself is a tribute to those fallen crumbs. For every trill mastered, for every clear pedal change, and for every gradient crescendo, we owe it to those pencil markings. We owe it to the old markings that you could probably still see if you held the page up to the sunlight. We owe it to the circles and curves, and numbers and lines, that helped us understand the music written two centuries ago. We owe it to the crumbs that, despite all efforts in cleaning them up, still lie in between the crevices of the score's ledge. The crumbs that never made it out, and the crumbs that still hold the markings that helped us achieve our performances.

Those eraser crumbs tell stories. They hold the truths of our hard work. They hold the realities of every struggle and every attempt. So lies the paradox: that although the crumbs hold our truths and our realities, they are indeed, erased from the page. In fact, by erasing the markings off the page, it is a sign of success. By removing the markings off the page, we symbolize our success and a notion of, "We don't need you anymore." But why would we forgo our truths? Why would we want to let go of the realities that are a part of who we are as musicians? If that's what we truly want to be, where does it leave us and what does that mean for the truth of being a pianist?

XXIII

fire

An image of perfection. An image of excellence. An image of, "hey I worked really hard at this now listen to me play." That's what I believe to be the truth of being a pianist. The way we best define the standards of "perfection" and "excellence" come from our due diligence of doing the composer justice—to pay homage to their time and their culture. To understand the ancestral developments of our instrument and the stylistic demands of the particular piece.

How does a pianist define success? How does one come to the conclusion that they've made it? Is it when we complete all examinations as per our curriculum requirements? Is it when we've won every competition we entered? Or is it when our piano teacher simply says, "good job." Success, in art, is subjective.

Some define success in the arts with a financial meter. The idea that the more gigs you have, the more students you have, the more money you have . . . the higher you've made it.

Some define success in the sense of how long you've been studying the piano. But that's hard too. I've played piano for almost twenty years, and there are those who've played only ten and seem to be more experienced than I. That's called talent, I guess.

Some define success with how well-"played" they are. Their experience with various genres and composers have given them the fruits of success and as a result accomplished a great deal in studying the piano.

None of those definitions are incorrect. That's why it's subjective. For me, it has always been the intensity of passion for the music and for the instrument(piano).

For me, it has always been the fire and the drive that you will one day possess when you sit on the bench in front of all eighty-eight of your musical friends. For me, success is when you've had a long day and you still haven't practiced piano, but it is not a feeling of dread but excitement.

To achieve and to improve in anything in life, we must have the inspiration and motivation to get better. We must have the fire to push ourselves to practice and work hard, and in time, we can start that fire within us.

My favourite part about this fire is that no one can truly feel it and see it quite as much as you will. Perhaps your hard work and a smile on your face may reveal it slightly. Perhaps your dedication to teaching and learning and performing may hint at your passion. Yet, you will feel it in your whole heart. You will feel the fire and the burning passion run through your veins, and straight to your fingertips with every note. You will feel it, I promise you.

The best part about this fire is that it will never die. In some points of your life you may feel it getting smaller because life has to happen, and you may have to put it on the backburner. So, you must fuel it. For when the fire gets smaller you will feel less of it, and sometimes, none of it at all. There will be moments where you've forgotten about this fire and that your entire life seems vacant of a special place in your heart. That's where the fire used to be. That's where the fire was burning in flames and now you've let it diminish. And that's okay.

For sometimes we need to let the fire go down a bit so we can realize that we need to fuel it again. Perhaps it means taking up lessons again. Maybe it means self-learning a new piece. Maybe it just means listening to some Mozart.

If you are a pianist reading this I encourage you to find your fire, if you haven't already. I encourage you to feel it with your entire being because that is the very purpose of our work and why we continue to choose to do what we do.

XXIV

mechanics

I will be honest, I don't quite know exactly how the piano works. I'm not familiar with its body parts, the mechanics inside, nor why the shape is the shape it is.

I also do not know much about the difference between brands, other than a Steinway feels better than a Kawaii, and a Yamaha is "softer" than a Petrof. I know that it is always better to have an acoustic piano and that a digital one comes nowhere near as valuable and rewarding. I also know that a piano is not truly a "piano" except for a grand or a baby grand; and that the shorter the strings are, the higher the pitch they will sound. In fact, it was only a few years ago that I learned truly what happens when the foot presses on each pedal.

I will not pretend like I have put an abundance of time to understanding the instrument. I am a mere student who just loves to play and teach; I do not know what most professionals and other students may know.

I asked around—friends, some colleagues, transfer students—and it seems that a lot of them do not know the things I mentioned earlier, either. It came to my attention, then, that perhaps there is a gap in our music education. It appears that piano studies are microscopically invested in understanding *performance* rather than *construction*. There is probably a perfectly sound explanation to this; something about how there will always be a price to pay for just how much one can learn with the instrument.

So during their study period, students learn to play a spectrum of pieces that summarize musical influences of human history. They even learn about cadential progressions, intervallic analysis, and harmonic construction. All the while, they have no course and no requirement to study the make-up of the very instrument they are learning about.

Which, unfortunately, leaves a huge disconnect between the artist and the canvas. It is as though the painting is presented but the canvas is left blank; or that the play has started but the stage is still empty; or that the sculpture is on display but the block of clay remains untouched. While the keys *give us* the pitches, and the pedal *gives us* the pitches, we may not know where it comes from. It's like never asking your mom about her childhood or buying a car from Kijiji without asking the mileage.

If you play piano, or any instrument, for that matter, I encourage you to explore the mechanics of that instrument. I encourage you to conduct a simple Google search where you'll be led to various YouTube videos, through articles and blogs that dive deep into how the piano works. In doing this, our art comes full circle. In doing this, we give our music a canvas—not for our audience, not for our teachers, but for ourselves. It is then we can understand its origin, its impact, and where it can go from there.

XXV

the first time

"We won't use those until later." Your teacher points to the *sostenuto* and *una corda* pedals as if there is caution tape plastered all across the left side of the pedal "dashboard." Learning piano, using the "pedal" has always meant only one thing: the damper. The damper pedal that makes the music sound as if the melody has been submerged underwater. Suddenly, the bass notes are deeper and more intense and your entire performance is upgraded to a sense of prestige. But what of the other pedals? You were always told not to use them and that you "won't use those until later" or that "we aren't using them right now." So you spend the first few years or your piano career avoiding the middle and left pedals, and dedicate your time to submerging your music underwater when necessary. "Con pedale" and "Ped" only means one thing and you would never try the others. You might sneakily try it at home when your teacher isn't there, but you never understood what they're for. No one cared to explain.

"Oh, that's the sostenuto." Whether you're at an upright or a grand, it wouldn't matter. Your teacher referred to your first time playing the sostenuto as though you were waking up to eat breakfast. Yet for some reason, you had expected some ceremonial process. Perhaps some fireworks to go off around you because up until now, the sostenuto was off limits.

"So you press it down like this, play the note, and voila!" Oh.

Shouldn't the process be a lot more special? Why do teachers treat playing the other pedals like a crime, yet when it comes to actually learning how to use them it's completely candid? Using the other pedals changes the entire sound of your music. It changes the way the different lines of music intertwine with each other. It changes the texture of the harmonies and it changes your physical response to playing the instrument. We must not take that for granted. Pianists, I believe, are products of their experiences with music and when we use a different pedal, we add-on to those experiences and grow even more.

So when you use the sostenuto or the una corda for the first time, take the time to see what happens. Take the time to truly appreciate the shift and difference in the sound, and do not be afraid to remove the lid off your piano to see what happens inside. Our response to our music is only as special as we make it.

Vignettes of a Pianist

XXVI

bookstore

The bells attached to the door hinge jangle and make a clattering sound. The store smells of paper, glue, and ink, and there's a faint buzz of the light fixtures that cover the entire ceiling. Like an upside-down carpet. You stomp your feet once, twice, three times over the mat to shuffle the snow off your boots so as not to "dirty" the carpet floor. In the midst of a heavy and cold winter, you're here. The music bookstore.

It is quiet inside. There are no conversations held more than the occasional exchange between the store associate and an inquiring customer. There is no more than the gentle tap between books as a customer flips through the new Christmas sheet music. You reach into your pocket to feel the yellow sticky note you folded up. Inside reads the three books you need to buy, as recommended by your teacher. Beethoven – B. Debussy – D. Mendelssohn – M.

All along the right side of the wall are scores in alphabetical order. Bach, you already know, is always near the back. If you wanted some more contemporary and pop pieces (like the songs you'd hear on the radio), you need not take more than a few steps inside the store because they're always at the front. The new Kelly Clarkson album has just been fully transcribed to a "Beginner's Piano" songbook, along with the "High School Music 3" movie soundtrack. As you pass by Kelly's face, and Zac Efron, and Vanessa Hudgens jumping for joy from graduation on the front cover, you hum a bit to yourself. Wishing you could play that for your exam instead.

The label that spells out "Bach" is faded. You know it was written with a black Sharpie because it has now faded to purple, and the masking tape where the ink lives is now frayed on the edges, as though some overnight music elf tried to remove it. To look for the Well-Tempered Clavier I and II (yes it's that time), you must turn your head a full 90 degrees, so you can read sideways. The owner of the shop puts cardboard dividers between the different volumes of Bach's work, so as to organize it in the best way he sees fit. It works.

The cardboard dividers are frayed on the edges and written in faded black Sharpie too. But you know it was written by the store owner because it's the same handwriting as the masking tape "Bach" label. Can you imagine how much time it must have taken him to label and categorize the entire store?

In these two cubbies of the store is where Johann Sebastien Bach lives. His music and almost all of his life's work nestles in between the faded Sharpie-written cardboard dividers, bound between editions and publications from every year in the twentieth to twenty-first century from almost every major city in the world.

Though J.S. Bach was born in Eisenach and spent much of his career in Leipzig, Germany, he now lives in almost every part of the world. In this instance, Bach lives in that small corner of the bookstore in between those cardboard dividers.

You flip through the dividers and notice that there's none for "Well Tempered Clavier." Yet under hiding behind the "Sinfonias" divider is the "Well Tempered Clavier" divider sitting upright. No wonder you couldn't see it. The previous customer must have played around with the books too much and upon putting back a book they didn't want, pushed the divider to sit upright like that.

When you've found both volumes of the "WTC," you bring it to the cashier to checkout. "Will that be all?" he asks. Well, no, technically not. Technically you could have unlimited funds to buy out the entire store and you'd still miss out on the music. Technically you could never have it "all" but for now, yes, it should be enough.

You push the door handle to leave and the bells jangle against each other, signalling your exit. Two books tucked under your arm and you feel the brisk wind hit your face. But inside you feel warm, you've just visited Bach. Plus, you get to take him home with you too.

Visits to the bookstore are sacred moments for a pianist's career. They are important and essential to expanding our physical library. But they are also moments for self-discovery and reconnections with composers of the past (and sometimes even present). For me, I recommend visiting a music bookstore alone—so you may discover and reconnect in private. So when you go home and open the new book up to the new piece you're starting, and push down the pages to bend the backbone of the book, you remember. You will remember that all it takes, sometimes, is a visit to the bookstore to remind you that more music exists out there; that the composers who have passed have actually left a piece of themselves with the world to enjoy and play. And it starts with you.

XXVII

watching

As the next performer walks up on stage, you can't help but feel a sense of gratitude and relief that it won't be you who is performing today. Today, you are just a spectator. Today, you are a part of the audience, looking from the outside in.

He takes a bow with one hand on the side of the grand and the other across his stomach. The audience claps as he takes a seat on the bench. His posture is almost flawless and his right foot slides over to the damper pedal. Prepared. His hands and fingers find their home bases on the keys and he takes a deep breath. Someone in the audience coughs. You take another look at the recital programme to double check what he's playing: a Chopin etude you're not familiar with.

He takes a deep breath and begins. His fingers flourish across the keys and they flutter like dragonflies zipping through tall blades of grass. A piece of his effortlessly gelled hair falls down and hits the front of his forehead. His eyes close at one of the sections and you, too, feel submerged in the music. Your eyes drift away from the sight of him and down to your lap. Though he is no longer in sight, the music continues.

Still looking down you suddenly hear him stop. Silence and another cough. You look up to check what's happened, and it appears to be the worst of all: he's blanked out. A memory slip and he is defeated. You can't help but want to run up the stage, give him a hug and tell him it's all going to be okay. In those three seconds your heart shakes as you remember the feelings of fear, regret, sorrow, anger, impatience, and defeat wrapping you up like a cocoon, so that the dragonflies your fingers were before have now vanished and have been swallowed up whole.

Instead, you keep your head down because by staring, you're useless. You look back down at the programme and for the sake of having nothing better to do, reread his name and the piece title. He then resumes playing just as if he broke out of the cocoon's finest thread. Thin and subtle, you could never really see the cocoon of fear and regret, but you would always feel it. Broken. Broken lay the remains of the cocoon, shattered into pieces, lying now on the floor of the stage while he continues to play on. Somehow and somewhere in his mind he had found his way back on the page in his mind. You wonder if it were perhaps a simple memory slip or just a brief trip of a note that snowballed into something unavoidably embarrassing. You wonder which part of him he feels the most: Was it regret? Shame? Fear? Was it the embarrassment of having to face his teacher after, or his dad who would look sternly at him? Was he regretting not practicing as consistently? No. He had probably played it through at least three times that morning, and practiced as much as he could in the weeks leading up to this moment.

The piece comes to a confident cadential close, and just like clockwork, just like the sun sets every day, and just as the leaves grow back in the spring, you and the rest of the audience lift your hands up for applause. He stands up, exhales a breath of what seems to be filled with a *melange* of relief and embarrassment, and takes a bow. Thank you, he seems to be saying, for putting up with that.

The truth is, the audience never has to "put up" with any performance. The truth is, all performances are beautiful in some way. Certainly not every performance is flawless; in fact, none of them ever are. The beauty of a live performance is that there is always an element of risk in that your piece could unfold as imperfectly perfect as you intended, or it could fall into complete shambles. There will always be a note amiss, a trill forgotten, a crescendo muted. There will always be too vague of a sixteenth-note run, too soft of a bass line, or even too strong of a final chord. There will always be a "something." The beauty in that, though, is that just like we refer to the cliché of one-of-a-kind snowflakes, and unique personalities, and homemade cookies, no two performances will ever be alike.

So we must omit the element of perfection when it comes to performing, and instead empathize with the artist on stage. We must try our best to feel for them. We must try to live the piece or song just as much as they have. After all, what is music without sharing?

XXVIII

(not) practicing

The printer turns on and you run over, waiting for the pages to spit out with a level of anticipation synonymous with waiting for lottery numbers. You've been listening to Jesse McCartney's "Beautiful Soul" in your mom's car on the way to school for the last three weeks now, and you finally found the sheet music online. It comes out eleven pages long. How does a piece that's typically only two minutes and forty-two seconds long, amount to eleven pages on the piano? And doesn't the chorus repeat?

You gather the last of the pages and enthusiastically run downstairs to your piano.

"Did you practice what you're supposed to practice yet?"

No, you hadn't. Here we go again, your mom bugging you because you hadn't practiced your exam repertoire and instead, spend your time frolicking around on Google trying to find the piano transcription of your celebrity crush's hit single, hopelessly trying to fill the void of feeling satisfaction from playing the piano.

"Ya, I'll get to it after this." That was probably the best response you could give her. You lay out the first four pages, since that's as much as the ledge will hold and you fumble to find the first few notes. The first four notes, typically played on the guitar are arranged here in a dotted rhythm format in conjunction with some syncopation and ties that you're not familiar with. Weird. Somehow you expected something a bit simpler . . . something easier to read. Suddenly it doesn't seem so appealing.

Well, you've printed it out so might as well try it. It is your favorite song, after all.

A few bars later and you begin to subtly recognize the opening tune . . . but something doesn't sound right. Sure, it's the same notes and the melody seems to be coming through. The lyrics printed underneath the notes are perfectly aligned so you can sing along, so you try your best. It just isn't the same.

Is this what it's like? To find piano sheet music and feeling let down? Isn't music supposed to be enjoyable? Fulfilling?

Frustrated, you gather up the rest of the sheets and set it aside. Suddenly uninterested and discouraged, you get up and walk away from the piano (again).

On a more rational note: yes, obviously the song would not sound the same on the piano. It wasn't even written for the piano. But somehow, your naïve self, your innocent musical mind thought that the piano was a magic instrument. That just because it holds all eighty-eight keys—which is virtually every pitch ever known to humankind—you could recreate any piece or song just by playing the right notes on the score.

I think the first time I learned that the piano wasn't magical I felt extremely discouraged.

I felt weakened because it was supposed to be my saving grace. I thought the piano would take me places without me trying. I depended on it for so many things in life: I depended on it for pleasure, imagination, creativity, success. Purpose.

I depended on it to quite literally define who I was. But did it? Can it?

No matter how much you come to recognize that the piano is an inanimate object, and incapable of reacting and responding to your voice and emotions, there is still, always, a glimmer of hope. That is because the connection that we as pianists develop with our instrument runs deeper than most human relationships ever could.

XXIX

missing out

"Sorry I can't, I have to go home and practice." Nine words that defined most of your life growing up. It never meant more than simply that no, you cannot go to the park after school because you have to go home and practice the piano. Nine words that, at the time and probably still does, limit you from having any sort of childhood or "fun." Nine words that you'd repeat over and over again, week after week, not knowing that one day, you'll finally be able to say, "Sure, I'll come."

It was never a choice either, right? It was not like you could actually ask your mom for permission and that maybe just today, just for one day, you could skip practicing or practice a little less so you could meet your friends after school. It was never a matter up for negotiation. It was always the one fact: that you must practice and you must do so after school before or after you finish your homework. No questions asked.

So in that moment, when you've spoken those nine words and you watch as your friends shrug with enough disappointment to last a maximum of sixty seconds, you wish you had another life. You wish that maybe, just for this once, you were not tied to go back home and practice and that you could just freely make a decision for yourself for once.

As you and your friends part ways–they to the park and you home, your head swings down like a broken bobble head on a car dashboard. Your backpack is heavy of homework, you feel a draft touch your skin because you didn't wear the warmer jacket that your dad had reminded you to that morning, and you are dreading the F minor scale you know you have to practice that day.

Alone. Your house is quiet because no one's home from work yet, and you feel the fridge buzzing as if to be your competitor for the incoming sound you're about to make on the piano. You throw your bag to the side of the hallway and wince, and you know you're not really supposed to do that. Your mind drifts to the park and thinking how much fun you're missing out on and what you'd do to be there right now, rather than sitting alone at the bench, again.

You don't cry though, and you're not particularly sad. No, you're not sad. This is not a sad moment and it's not meant to be. It's more a mix of disappointment and longing. But not sadness. You were never sad that you had to go home and practice because at the end of the day, you knew what was best. You knew that you'd have an exam coming up at the end of this August and that you hadn't even started to memorize your waltz yet. You knew that if you didn't get a good mark on this exam you'd waste your parents' money on these expensive piano lessons and books—and boy were they expensive.

So it's fair to say that you'd never regret these moments. You'd look back on these days several years from now and remember not the disappointment and longing, but the strength and progress that you've accumulated. You'll remember not the look on your friends' face or the feeling of dread as you walked home alone, but the confidence and skill that you've built up. You'll remember those moments of loneliness as moments of pride because you accomplished it alone and you have only one person to thank: yourself (and your parents too, never forget about them).

Progress is lonely, and so is success. We know these feelings for its entirety because we share it with no one but ourselves. When we reject our friends, when we opt out of fun outings or leave the lively dinner conversations early, we surrender for our art. When we tell others "sorry I can't" and "maybe next time," we are not missing out. We must remember that our commitment to the piano is more than just practicing. It is actively participating in a virtually bound contract between you and other pianists that you will commit to the instrument, as it does for you.

the chair

If you're lucky, you'd get a cushioned one. Most of the time, though, it would be one of those black fold-up chairs; the ones that could collapse if you move around on it too much because it's lopsided.

"Sit here and wait until the examiner calls you." They're always nice, those girls and guys who walk you to the chair. They're nice because the extent of their job stops there. They don't have to sit on that chair and wait. They don't have to anticipate what's behind that door. Most of all, they don't have to get up from the chair and walk into that room.

You nod and watch as they walk away, back down the hall in a pace that signifies that there's no rush at all. Your exam is scheduled for precisely 10:36am and it's now 10:34am. You're right on time and they've done their job.

As they round the last corner they disappear completely and now it's just you, an empty hall, a closed door, and the chair. You search for distractions and you notice a cheesy canvas print hanging from the wall.

Music is Life

You can't help but wonder if whoever bought this at the time truly believed in this, or did they just need some cheap wall art to fill up the empty space on the sad walls that barricaded the rooms of doom? At least, that's what it seems like at the moment. You can't help but imagine what goes on in those rooms when it's not exam season. Lessons? Theory classes? Or space for extra storage? It's amazing how one room can fulfill so many purposes at different occasions. yet house musicians that feel the same way all the time: joy, defeat, and the most famous one, the endless feeling of never being "enough."

The next thing you notice is that there's a short printed biography of your examiner stuck to the door of the examination room. It's black and white, of course, to save money. No one funds the arts, right? You read and try to pronounce the examiner's name in your head—just in case you feel like addressing them later on. Won't' be necessary though. And because you have nothing better to do, you start to read their biography. You can tell by the rhetoric that it was probably copied from some website that the examiner had funded at one point, but forgot to update it at least five years ago. Nonetheless, they are still ornately decorated with degree after degree, honor after honor, colored with popular city names where they've performed. Their picture is probably outdated too, and you notice how proper and even scary they may look. You find yourself having a sudden admiration and even envy towards their job—that they've taken something they know and love and turned it into a full blown career. Astounding.

You search your surroundings for any indication of what time it might be. There's not a single clock in sight and of course you wouldn't be wearing a watch. Your heart starts to race because you know the time is nearing, and there's truly nothing more you can do to salvage how you'll do. Your mind wanders to one of your pieces, your Mendelssohn. A part of your mind starts humming it but you quickly brush the melody away–the last thing you need is to cultivate a breeding ground for a memory slip. You look down and your repertoire books are staring right back at you. The painted scene of pastoral England, or somewhere in the northern United Kingdom, stares right back at you. You've seen this painting on the front cover a countless amount of times already, but somehow you've never noticed the yellow flowers dotted in the background. Were they always there? You probably never bothered to pay enough attention because you were too busy finding your way to your pieces. It's amazing how much we miss in the midst of chasing after something else. Even though what we miss is so undeniably visible and obvious, it's like our minds purposely reject and detach from our immediate surroundings, all the while missing out on what could be important. Still, staring at the painting more time passes by. What seemed like over five minutes was probably only forty seconds. If you look close enough, you can see the many different shades of green the artist used for grass. The strokes are clear enough to dissect, and in between the darker and lighter greens you realize where true beauty can be found: in between the smallest of details and most narrow of differences. It is all beautiful.

Your eyes glance a bit to the right, to the bookmarks poking out of the pages marked "one," "two," "three." This was to make sure the examiner could turn to each piece as quickly as possible. Because of course, why would you want to waste their time?

So in the midst of your racing heart, analysis of the numbered bookmarks, and the empty corridor, you hear it. The sound of the door knob turning creaks next to your left ear, and you know what's coming next. There was a turn, a fidget, and one full 360 degrees completed later, the previous student walks out, head down, and you know it's your turn.

"Come on in!" You look up at the examiner, not at all what you'd expect her to be. You know that there's no time to waste and even though it's well past 10:36am, you still have to walk in there and conduct every portion expected of you.

And so you get up from the chair and walk into the room, with no one but you and that chair sharing the last four minutes together. The experience of waiting for something so uncertain and lonely. The moments that strengthen us as musicians. What remains just as profound is that that chair is an endless servant. It remains there, lined up against the wall of the hallway, waiting for the next person, to begin yet again, another four minutes of waiting. Or more.

XXXI

one question, many answers

"So how's piano going?"

What is that even supposed to mean? Well, at least they asked. Sometimes you would be lucky to even get asked. Here, "piano" is synonymous with the very act of playing and learning the piano, but not the actual instrument itself. Semantics.

To summarize an extremely time consuming, physically challenging, and emotionally draining part of your life with simply the word for the tool that helps you get there—how diminishing. Though it's not meant to be. It's only diminishing because you have no idea how to even begin to answer this question. For instance, what aspect of the "piano" would they be referring to? The part where you were supposed to have your Sonatina memorized two days ago but haven't? The part where your theory homework is sitting underneath your desk because it fell on the floor last week and you still haven't picked it up? Or the part where you have so much homework there is absolutely no time to practice, yet you have your lesson tomorrow? Or, is it the part where Christmas is coming soon and you're finally excited to play "Grown Up Christmas List" for the fifth year in a row?

"It's good."

That's all you have the courage to spit out. In all honesty, it *is* good you suppose. It's definitely not going badly, that's for sure. At least, you don't think it is. The thing is, it's not their fault for asking. It's no one's fault. But what lies behind the word "piano" are blankets and blankets of challenges and moments of hard work that are worth way more than the span of a four-worded question. You wish for once that there might be some person who would ask you "How are you liking playing piano?" or "How do you find practicing these days?"

The problem is people don't see the value in learning the piano as much as they see going to a math tutor or swimming lessons. Taking music lessons is "superfluous" to most. So we fear. We fear that we may be looked down on. We fear that what we have to offer is inadequate and will always come secondary to whatever else is being taught in the world.

So they ask and wonder, but truly it's out of courtesy. And that's fine, but to say that we are invincible to the let-downs of our immediate community's curiosity, to our musical well being—well, we're not.

XXXII

mind travelling

What do you hear when you play the piano? A band teacher once told me that playing music is 20% actual playing and the other 80% is listening. But on the piano we hear nothing but our own part, and for that alone sometimes, may deafen our abilities to focus, and most of all, listen.

As a pianist, how often do you hear your own music while playing? When you record yourself, it's always easy to evaluate and listen from that. But when you're performing or practicing, how much of each hand can you devote your attention to? Most of all, what goes on in your mind?

The power of muscle memory allows us as pianists to detach ourselves from our music every so often. That is to say, if we know a piece well enough, our fingers do the work for us, and our minds can afford to wander off. Wander where, though? Typically for me, I go off to a creative space. For me, a creative space is where I brainstorm the best and worst of my ideas. In my creative space, I explore all imagined possibilities, and there, I am limitless.

I once told my teacher, by accident, that I do this. I let it slip by accident that I actually know the piece so well that I do not need to be thinking about it all the time. I think she told me to count properly and I completely dismissed her by telling her that I don't actually think about the piece when I'm playing it. She was horrified. Shocked. It was then when I realized I guess I was not supposed to do that.

Although my creative space was discouraged at an early stage of my piano studies, I could never help but travel there from time to time. Sure, as a more mature musician, I now have more control where my mind goes. But I feel that in moments of practicing and rehearsing, a bit of mind travelling won't hurt. Mind travelling when playing the piano is a healthy task, I think. I think it helps our minds generate ideas and understand that something beautiful can come from another beautiful thing. I think mind travelling tests our stamina to just how long we can think and do two (sometimes three things) at once. I think mind travelling is good for our mental health.

I don't speak much on mental health because I am not an expert on it. I have been blessed that I don't experience negative episodes of mental health issues in my life, but I've had my moments. Practicing mind travelling whilst playing the piano, I think, is what contributed to my ability to stay grounded everywhere else in life.

I pray that whoever you are reading this, that you remember to find your creative space once in a while. As pianists, we can find the creative space while we sit on the bench, letting our hands flourish and run back and forth down the keys. We can think about new projects we want to do, dreams we want to chase, careers we want to go for when we are in the creative space. In this space, we can think of ways to solve a conflict with a friend, a new restaurant you might want to try on the weekend, or how best to tell your mom you're grateful for her. In this space, your thoughts are your own and you are not judged for who you are and what you do.

There is something wildly peaceful about being in your own space. Oftentimes, we describe peace as a space of quiet and tranquility. But peace is whenever I am playing. Peace is when I am in my creative space. There is a certain equilibrium that you reach when you play and wander your mind. Search for it.

XXXIII

hunting

As human beings, there is always a part of us that searches for community. We yearn for the comfort of knowing someone else feels the same way we do. We hope that we can be relatable for others and them to us. But sometimes, it is safer and oftentimes more rewarding to be alone.

While community and a pleasant circle of musical friends is comforting we must learn to exist on our own as musicians. Being a pianist, I think, helps you find treasures that you could otherwise not find should you do it with someone else. Let me tell you about some of my own treasure hunting experiences.

Tone.

I did not learn about tone production until much later in my piano studies. I wish I had learned it earlier, actually. Nonetheless, when the idea that pressing "deep" into the keys and letting the intention "travel" from your arm to the tip of your fingers became a reality to me, I took it upon myself to listen for the tone that everyone else was talking about.

It started with a single note. I think I chose E, the one closest to middle C. I played the tone down with my second (index) finger on my right hand and heard the sound. I pressed "into" the key and listened. Too harsh. Too soft. Too much. How was I supposed to get it?

It took me a few tries, but I finally ended up achieving the perfect balance between pressing deep into the key while keeping a strained effect on the sound production of a single note. The feeling was irreplaceably rewarding and I will never forget that moment.

Up the mountain.

There was a period in my piano career where I felt completely unmotivated and uninspired with the musical world. I had close to zero interest in learning, and practicing was a burden I carried with me on a daily basis. Just the thought of having to go to a piano lesson on Tuesdays made a part of me feel heavy and I dreaded it to the last second. I stopped caring altogether about my process. In conjunction, I was in the midst of my teenage angst and completely unready to face the impending "real world," coupled with everyday high school drama, and trying to get the solo in the jazz band with my mediocre saxophone skills. Needless to say, I was not at a high point.

So when I finally found a teacher who truly inspired me to love music again, I was ready to dive back into the piano. Suddenly, it was a magnetic pull that led me to practice every night. I, along with my parents, was not ready to let that go to waste.

There was a pivotal moment in one of these newly inspired practicing sessions where I was in the midst of a bar, and I felt this sudden burst of energy that made me realize just how much music meant to me. It was as close to magic as I could ever get. It was like suddenly the war of practicing and going to lessons had been dismissed from my universe. For those three seconds it was just me, my fingers, and the music.

In learning to play, we will always seek community. There is no denying that we need the comfort from others in order to feel like we are doing something right. And that's fine. But what is most important to remember is that oftentimes, if not always, the best and most rewarding moments are those experienced alone. We must be brave and strong enough to fight through the tides of "loneliness," and instead bask in the magical moments that solitude can bring. We should hold on to the moments where we sit on the bench, by ourselves, reading through the music that seems so impossible yet only a few weeks away from being memorized by your muscles. We shall never forget these moments because they cannot be shared. They are treasures that are enclosed in our hearts. They are miniature moments that are truly, wholeheartedly, and completely our own. Why? Because from start to finish, we experience them by ourselves. That, in itself, is worth treasuring.

XXXIV

tabletops

Where there's a hard surface, your hands will curve. Like typing on a laptop, playing a video game, or texting, any machine that resembles the piano keyboard is a natural invitation to assume the position to start a piece. When you're sitting at a desk with nothing to do, you're ghosting your fingers, and tapping and hitting the table like you're giving a full performance. When your hands are wrapped around the steering wheel and just after the right turn, when your fingers find themselves nestled on top of the honk button, they start to tap. And even when there's no hard surface, even when you're not sitting at a table, but you're waiting in your doctor's office in that painfully quiet room—you turn to your lap. Though cushioned by the make-up of your body, you still find a way to play.

The most ironic part about ghost playing is that no sound ever comes out; which is probably why it's called "ghost" playing. But why do we still do it? Though we yearn to create music and find the joy in hearing the melody that we've worked on countless times already, we still crave the feeling of "playing." The very act of curving your palms, curling your fingers, and moving them profusely to mimic the effect of playing is somehow satisfying. That we do not need the sound of the keys to make us feel at home, and instead find solace on tabletops.

XXXV

glissandos

What would otherwise be a careless scribble signifies a feature that tells people: yes, you can play the piano. If there were only a few distinct ways to identify a "very good" pianist to the untrained ear, the *glissando* could be among them. The upward (sometimes downward) movement on the keys should be swift, smooth, and effortless, shouldn't it? But it seems that the first time we learn it, the keys hit the roots of our cuticles and debunk the glorified effect of the glissando. What is otherwise impressive and a landmark of our technical and stylistic abilities, is at first painful and a stumbling journey across the octaves. We are not superheroes, we cannot create sounds with the piano on the first try, and I think that's what we forget sometimes.

Playing a glissando reminds me that like most things in life, we need to work at it. In other words, for something to be smooth, flawless, and effortless, we must first put in the rough and imperfect work, and with tons and tons of effort. Just because we have a scribble across the last measure does not mean it won't take time to perfect. What often seems the simplest and most trivial, are often the most time consuming and taxing of our capabilities.

But fear not, because glissandos, when done well, are impressive. They impress people to the point where even if you've been studying the piano for just three months, their eyes widen and jaws drop. They don't ponder about whether or not you've produced the right tone or kept a consistent beat. They do not question your ability to read music quickly or whether you've used the pedal in a logical and natural manner. All that matters is that gliding sound of the back of your fingers across the keyboard. All that matters is that you can show many sounds and flourishes as possible in the span of three seconds. Voila.

XXXVI

maintenance

Short, unpainted fingernails. Such are the recommendations by every piano teacher. Just how many students will follow these guidelines? Very few. It is so challenging, I think, for a student to make that commitment to the instrument. It is unlike practicing where you make an active decision to incorporate it into your routine. It is unlike learning new music where you dedicate time to exploring the sounds and rhythms of an artistic world. It is even unlike the added pressures of success that is often packaged in the same space as learning music.

Well maintained fingers are a commitment that many students do not want to adhere to because, well, there just isn't enough reason to do so. If at the beginning a student practices twenty minutes a day, six days a week (as they should be doing), and thirty minutes of lesson on the seventh day, that is only a total of 150 minutes out of the 604,800 that we have in a week. That's only about 0.02% of the week. Is having to keep your nails short and stopping self expression through painted nails worth this?

I'm not here to tell you whether or not it actually is, because that's not what this book is about. But I'll tell you about a time it made me realize that it is, indeed, worth it.

At the tail end of my middle school years I, like most teenagers, was rebelling against any rule or guideline ever formed by an adult. I did everything in my power to make sure that my mom never won an argument and my piano teacher never had the satisfaction of my abidance. So, I painted my nails.

To most, that seems extremely trivial and worthless to even write about. Well, for me, it was a big deal. I still remember I had painted my nails a pale purple color. My best friend at the time was obsessed with this color and because I was also obsessed with the concept of fitting in, I did so anyway. I painted my nails, knowing that I wasn't supposed to and practiced piano with it.

I don't want to say that it was a dramatic blow up because I had "rebelled" against this informal rule when taking piano lessons. There was no argument, no tears, and definitely no blood involved. Instead, I noticed that just after a day of piano practice, my nails had already chipped. It was that day that I realized that my vanity was not worth it. Like some girls growing up, I was always into the idea of what we now call "self care." I liked to have pretty nails and pretty hair, and begged my mom to buy me all the pretty clothes. I realize now that she often did not buy me the trendiest clothes because she needed the money to pay for my piano lessons. I am grateful she had her priorities straight and that she did not listen to my silly self.

From my chipped nails, I remembered just why they were chipped in the first place. It was not because I had tried to open a box, or ran it against the tree bark at recess. It was not because I fell down in gym class or was doing some intense workmanship in design and tech class. It was because I was practicing piano. It was because I was working hard at something that I would one day love the most. At the time, I did not love it. But I did see the value in it.

The thing is, when you work hard at something, other things are worth sacrificing. My chipped nails were a symbol of my hard work and dedication to my art. My chipped nails were proof that I had been practicing. They were proof that rebelling against that informal rule of "keep your nails bare" was not at all worth it. It didn't even look good.

So it was then that I concluded perhaps I could not have both. Perhaps I could not have the luxury of having nicely painted nails while also practicing vigorously night after night. I needed to sacrifice one, and I guess I chose the piano.

It was also a struggle, I admit, to maintain short nails. I would have to set daily reminders to cut my nails so they would not make that embarrassingly click-clack as I played for my teacher every week. It was so embarrassing I feel ashamed just thinking of it right now. I would feel ashamed because she'd remind me, too. Every week she would tell me that I would need short nails so as long as I decide to play. Every Monday night I'd forget; and every Tuesday I'd feel the embarrassment. I was embarrassed because I knew what had to be done. I knew that I should have cut them but I guess I was always too lazy to care and too tired to remember. Looking back, I fear that such a small thing as not cutting my nails had actually hindered my development as a musician.

XXXVII

helpless

"Coming up . . . one more bar . . ." and you nod. The page turner gets up from their seat, but doesn't straighten their body because they don't need to. All they have to do is offer up half a second of their non-sitting time to flip a page for you, so you may continue on with the music.

If only we always had the luxury of a page turner with us all the time.

"Play for us!" You open the book that you haven't seen since the last time someone told you to "play for them." The spine is thick and stiff from little usage, and for the next two minutes it is a battle between you and the book, trying to straighten it and flatten it down as much as possible, so you can sit down and play the music freely, without needing anyone to help you.

It's December twenty-fourth, Christmas Eve, and you're told to play "Grown Up Christmas List" for the first time since, well, last Christmas Eve. You look at the music with double sixths and a minimal baseline, and begin to sight read. How sad, you think to yourself, that you're able to sight read this piano cover of Kelly Clarkson's rendition, while the works of Bach and Hanon are moved aside to be nothing but paper weights to keep the book from moving.

You continue to play and as you approach the end of the second page, you have to turn the page. Midway through the melody, you cut it off to get up and turn the page and make sure that Bach isn't flying off the ledge. As you do this, your family stands around you, watching, staring blankly and not trying to help. Not because they don't want to or not that they aren't supportive, but because they simply just don't know what to do.

So for a few moments of silence as you struggle to keep the page flattened against the ledge, pressing down as hard as you can the arch of the pages, you feel a sudden sense of guilt. The guilt that reads, "I should have photocopied this earlier" or "I'm sorry I don't know it well enough to not use the book" or "I just don't play it often enough to have the pages remember to bend.

The thing is, it's all fine. No one is truly judging you and no one is truly thinking poorly of you. After all, we are our biggest critics. As pianists, we feel bad when we do not deliver and execute to a socially acceptable standard. Our guilt eats us up when we don't play the right notes or adhere to the correct key signature (four sharps – what??). We hate having to have a non-appointed page turner and we, above all else, hate not being able to play the pieces that are supposed to be easily sight read.

I don't have all the answers or any answer, for that fact. I only know my answer. When we can't fulfill the task of playing a simple piece to our family members, we feel as though we've failed as pianists. We haven't completed our purpose. At the end of it all, we just want to share music, right? So what good are we if we can't deliver music that our loved ones want from us? Sure, we can play a *prelude* and *fugue* with no mistakes and highlighting every voice, but we can't even sight read the "Sound of Music" without mistakes? How do we even call ourselves musicians?

Many could say the solution to this would be to just simply practice more. Practice the pieces that your friends and family would request from you every Christmas. Prepare a binder full of sheet music, with tunes that people would actually know. Would that be the answer? Would that help us solve our problems of embarrassment and guilt every time our friends come over? We could try, but I'm not so sure if that would help us feel fulfilled. It's an experience that comes with the job, I think. It's a price to pay. It is the price to pay if you decide to embark on a serious journey of piano studies, trying your best to perfect pieces in the Baroque, Classical, and Romantic eras. We can't have it all, can we?

XXXVIII

wedding

As musicians in first world countries, we take many luxuries and privileges for granted. Among them, is the privilege of having a beautiful acoustic piano to practice and play on. If you have an upright or grand acoustic at home right now, consider yourself extremely privileged for this. If you have the fortune to practice on an acoustic piano every night before bed, or even have a piano to play on at choir rehearsals, you are luckier than many others.

My first time playing for a wedding, I was given an electronic keyboard. I remember this very vividly because the feeling of the keyboard still vibrates under my fingertips if I choose to relive it. I sat at the back of the ceremony and there was a full eighty-eight, semi-weighted keyboard in front of me. I felt honoured and privileged to be asked to play at this wedding, and I genuinely was not disappointed that I did not have a proper acoustic to play on. I wasn't disappointed because it made me realize something.

As the lights around me dimmed to pink and the smell of flowers weaved through the air of the room, I opened up my music. It was your typical wedding music, nothing of interest to me. I struggled to have the binder balance perfectly on the stand, and wobbled on the make-shift bench I was sitting on. I sat back down and started to play what I had been practicing for the last two months. I realized, then, that the term "semi-weighted" was extremely accurate, and not at all what I expected. My first thought was, regrettably, "Oh gosh, I don't deserve this." Quickly brushing away my toxic trait of acting entitled, I remembered why I was there. Two months ago I was asked to be a pianist for the wedding of two individuals close to me. Why should I feel annoyed simply because I wasn't given the proper instrument?

 It's important to remember that although the weight of the keys was not what I was used to, or that the music stand didn't balance my music perfectly, or that the bench was not sturdy enough, the most valuable aspect was that my music was invited. It was my music because along with my presence, so was my gift to share music with the rest of the wedding. That in itself is so special.

 So in a way, the all-too-light weight of the keys and the dull sound of the electronic keyboard is a symbol that music, regardless of when and where, is still music. No music is more sacred than another, and your privilege of playing on a beautiful instrument at home is not a measurement of what you deserve.

 Remember that your music is yours and what you're given to share it with is secondary. Meaning, the instrument is your privilege and your skill is your gift. The perfect combination, therefore, is to find the balance of cherishing the instrument and your skill, wrapped in nothing but passion for the art that you live for.

XXXIX

a secret

As a pianist, your music is not always with you. Meaning, unlike a violin or trumpet, your music can only exist where there exists a piano. So instead, typing an intense email to a client, playing a speed skill testing iPhone game, or even fidgeting with the controls of your new car—those are instances where the echoing movements of your fingers come to life. Your fingers are only fingers until they make music. They are not sources of music until you hit the black and white keys, and the most terrifying reality of them all, is no one would never know you're a musician until you sit down at that bench. No one. Being a pianist is a secret until you've actually played a piano. You can tell people all you want. You can share your story a million times over, but until you've positioned yourself in front of all eighty-eight hammers, you're a mystery to those around you and that is what gives artists the power that we often overlook.

But isn't that the point of communication? To share your passion? If piano is a part of who you are, and if music is the ingredient that runs through your veins and keeps you sane and at peace with the tragedies and terrors of the world, we must remind those around us constantly. Not because we seek to annoy them or because we think they may forget. But because we must be advocates for our own story. We must be the representatives of our silent fingers and mute hearts. We must be the messengers for which our passion remains unheard and the voice for all those who have never been as fortunate. We must.

I like to believe that the message is more powerful than the person. By logic, that would mean that the pianist is not as important as the music that he/she creates. The performance always trumps the performer. The score always precedes the actor. Always. I say this because humans are vessels for judgment. We invite others to judge us without even trying, and we always, always, create an inevitable breeding ground for discouragement. But the music? The score? The notes themselves? They are always there. They do not fight back, they do not call back. They do not even try to raise their point. When the composer is finished and when the copies have been printed, the music is separated from its creator. It exists as its own entity and we must preserve it by promoting it through ourselves, yet always assume an inferior position.

XL

competition

Page two. What comes after the F? Blankness. Nothingness. He's almost done playing so it'll be your turn in under ninety seconds. You know this because you played this piece three months ago, and you were awful at it. He's brilliant at it. You should have brought an extra copy to review on your lap. But then your hands would be cold. Then you'd forget about your gut. Applause roars around you and he gets up from the bench to take a bow. What's the point anyway? We know he already won.

"Next." Yes, that's you. You're next. Are you ready? No. You have no idea what note comes after the first page, the photographic memory your mind has managed to develop, completely blanked when it came to the second page, and now you're going to have to manage the following five with the utmost confidence. Hands start to shake, and you've got nothing left but your gut. There's still an ounce of hope inside you that maybe your fingers will remember for you. I mean, they're the ones doing all the work, right? The room is silent as they await your grand entrance, as you step up to the stage and take your first bow. You can't help but look forward to when this would all be over; and by this, you mean when the entire "taking piano lessons" part of your life is over. Little do you know.

Your sweaty palm meets the edge of the black vinyl finished instrument and you take your first bow. The audience claps again, signalling "let's get a move on." You take a seat and there it is, once again, the set of eighty-eight. You saw the same set only forty-five minutes ago in your own home, but why does it suddenly feel so foreign? It's like when you go back to school in September to a new classroom with the exact same layout and furniture, just one door over. It's like ordering a California roll at three separate sushi restaurants, but the crab meat quality is different three separate times. Tastes the same though.

You finally manage to lace your fingers in between the keys, and you start. Melodies flourish and chords enter, but the second page is still a mystery to you. The last cadence before that treble F is coming up and you still have no idea what happens next. Suddenly, the middle of the second page pops into your head. The notes begin to materialize and maybe, maybe, there is a sliver of hope. So for the next three bars you hold onto that sliver, and you put your entire faith into your fingers' guts that they'll deliver when necessary. As though you've prepared for this moment seven months before, and that you woke up extra early this morning to review, and that your mom even paid for an extra lesson this week, perhaps you won't make that all go to waste.

The F sounds and you have nothing. Your hands freeze and your mind goes blank. The room spins and your heart drops. Your feet pause and you feel your face burn red, and every pair of eyes remains on you, expectant of the next move. Your next move. But you have nothing to offer. You have nothing to give and nothing to fill that void that you've left alone because of a reason you'll never figure out. You feel the pressure of your mom, teacher, yourself, caving in on you, and you feel the remorse and regret that I'll unfold for the next several weeks. All that you have left, is the last two lines of the second page. Those miraculous last few lines that your memory gracefully offered back to you.

I never understood the source of blanking out. I thought I had always practiced enough and I thought I had always paid enough attention. But in reality I really didn't. The truth is, there is no regret nor remorse necessary for this. There is no need to cry and doubt and feel anxious because you blanked out for five seconds during a piano competition fourteen years ago. There is no need because in the grand scheme of every musical vignette you'll ever live through, that will never climb to be the defining moment of your success, and which makes you the musician that you are. We can try all we want to understand why we fail and why we forget the music in those moments. But where would that take us? Would understanding the core of the problem prevent it from happening time and time again? Would that help us become better musicians?

XLI

ear

There is an unspoken expectation that all good musicians must also have good ears: whether this is from perfect pitch, sight singing, or just good audio memory. Sometimes, those qualities can be trained through careful preparation in time and hard work. Most of the time, though, they either come naturally or they do not.

So what happens if you're unfairly dealt the cards of a passion for music yet with little talent, then what are you supposed to do?

I believe that untalented but dedicated musicians reveal the most about the capabilities of human beings. It is the unbalanced equation of two qualities that just don't seem to be the right fit together but somehow, the majority of students just do not have the natural awareness for rhythm and sound.

As children, if we are discovered to be any less talented or blessed with musical genes, the first instinct is to remove us from that world. It is the notion that if we are not good at something, then we must not like it. What happens, then, if you happen to love something you are not good at?

Pianists are praised all the time for being accomplished and "talented" because they have a museum of framed diplomas and trophy tokens sitting on their mom's living room shelf, collecting dust. Others around them seem to have this mythological belief that as long as you have a stack of papers, gold trinkets, and a performance of "Fur Elise" to show, then you're good to go. You're set to be a "really good pianist."

The trouble is, these are all just a part of the packaging. Consider this: a student who finishes all the required levels with the Royal Conservatory of Music, and even goes on to completing the performance diplomas. For the last fifteen years, this student has spent at least four to five hours a week practicing, never failing an exam. And so with a pass, they receive a diploma, and another reason for dad to buy a frame and nail another hole in the wall. Every once in a while, they'll participate in a competition in April, and they'll win second place three times, and third place five times. The local school they take lessons at recognizes their achievement every year, for their dedication to not only the instrument, but also, of course, their parents unending supply of financial support.

This student is hard working but not talented. This student is dedicated but not bright. This student participates but never takes the limelight.

Is this fair? Is this fair in comparison to the other, more "talented" individuals who wish to be in the limelight but are, in reality, outshone by the more hard working? Passion is not concurrent with success.

For me, this gives me a great sense of relief. It gives me a sense of relief because it reminds me that music and learning music is accessible. It is accessible to the talented, accessible to the passionate, and without a doubt, accessible to the hard working.

Your audio talents and gifts are not limited to what you can and cannot do. It is more about how much work you want to put into it. So the next time you're at a competition or you see someone on YouTube who seems much better than you are, do not be discouraged. There is much more than the final product, and giving a good performance is not an accurate depiction of a pianist's capabilities, or lack thereof.

XLII

myth

A myth we tell ourselves, or more often others tell us, is that we are all special. We're told we're unique, one-of-a-kind, irreplaceable. But what we all quickly learn, as we burst out into the real world after the safety net of closed academic institutions, we are not at all special. In fact, our similarities with other people are what defines us and then it is a matter of what category we fit into.

This is all not to say that we are not worthy or capable. I think it would be a great injustice to lie to ourselves that we are all "special" because in the end, we share similar goals and values in life.

Community

Love

Closure

Kindness

And because we share so much sameness, it is only logical to say that we are all connected in some way; and to recognize that connection, we have music.

Music is a universal art and language easily understood by all. We need not use words or actions, only sound. Over time, music has been passed down through the course of tradition and ritual, serving as the distinct basis of every culture. We use music to heal, to pair with moving pictures, to dance to, to fill in silences, to entertain, to earn money, to build character, to improve skills. We also use music to connect.

In a single instant, we can be connected through the art of sound. From a single melody, we can be wrapped by the same song. From a single song, we can embark on the same ship that sails down the staves of this universal language.

So it is not us as humans who are each special. It is our music that makes us special. As the performer, as the conductor, the composer, or even the listener.

XLIII

the weight

The audience claps and you stand up to take a bow. The claps rustle through your ears like the beating of human drums, filled with encouragement and gratitude. It was an alright performance: a few trips here and there, a memory slip that was going to happen but didn't, and an all too loud, perfect cadence at the end of the Exposition. But you made it through. Sound. Alive.

The claps die down as your eyes move from staring down at the stage floor and back up to the audience. Emotionless. As you turn towards the steps to walk down the stage the claps disappear completely. All that is left is the growing screams of the impatience of the next performer, waiting to do a slow run up the stage and do what you just did, all over again. You feel the spotlight escape you as you near the top of the stairs, feeling something you have not felt in a long time: freedom. Suddenly, stage fright and memory slips are foreign concepts to you. Suddenly, you need not lie in bed night after night, worrying of what "might" happen or what "should" happen. It is over now.

You make your way down the stairs and weave through the seats to find where your purse is sitting. Your dad looks up at you and gives your arm a reassuring and congratulatory squeeze. You look over at your mom to gauge some sort of response or emotion; nothing. She doesn't even turn to look at you, as though you never even left that stage, and that the empty bench on stage is actually still holding up your body. She does not look at you because she knows. She knows about the missed B, the almost memory slip, and the too strong cadence. She heard it all and she has convinced herself that your performance was anything but flawless, and you'll pay for it later.

You take your purse and sit down at the chair, checking to see the time. Eight minutes passed since you left the chair to go on the stage. In just eight minutes, your world shifted, and the entire body shed off the weight that burdened you for the last three months. Was it worth it? Was the performance worth it? Was it worth it to hold onto that weight of fear and anxiety for all this time? For a quarter of a year you did not sleep peacefully at night. All for those eight minutes.

At that moment you may have felt like it was not. At that moment it feels like it was all for nothing because in the end, you still made mistakes, and you still gave a less than perfect performance. What you may have forgotten, however, is what you were able to share. For in this dark, scary, dangerous, and uncertain world, for eight minutes straight you offered a light. For eight minutes you brought sensitivity and creativity into the world, and brightened it. By offering a part of your hard work and accomplishment in the form of music, you've lit up the skies after sunset and shone rays through the caves of uncertainty.

The message is more powerful than the person. We are more than just the wrong notes we play or how we convey the loudness of a *forte*. We are more than our memory slips and long passages. We are couriers of a greater message, which is to bring light with our music, whether in a one hour's practice, a fifteen minute jam session with friends, or an eight minute less-than-perfect performance.

XLIV

the wait

The wait begins the moment you leave the room.

"Thank you for coming," they say. But no thanks for making me wait at least three weeks for my results. For the next twenty-one days, refreshing the website for my mark will be the first and last thing I do every few hours. For the next twenty nights, my sleeps will be clouded with uncertain thoughts and worst case scenarios. It happens every time and every time you are not prepared for it.

There is a certain way to measure this feeling. It is measured, I believe, through the amount of attention you give to your daily life within these twenty-one days. It is measured by how many times in between, checking for the mark, does your mind wander off to the aftermath of finding out the pass or fail. Regardless of how often, though, the feeling has no filter or regard of when it happens.

You could be lying on a beach in Malibu, and suddenly the sunny day turns grey for a few moments as your mind re-enacts the way you played that scale.

You could be eating at your favorite Thai restaurant with your favorite person, and suddenly nothing about the environment is your favorite as an unexpected wave of indifference hits you over the head, and you cannot help but recall the awful way you recovered from your missed accidentals.

You could be at work in a meeting, discussing an upcoming project, which you were the core thought leader of, and suddenly you are thrown into the backseat, playing the underdog. Your swivelling ergonomic chair becomes the leather covered piano bench, and the boardroom tabletop is the keyboard. Your hands hover over it because you've momentarily forgotten where the piece begins.

It is like a heavily weighted blanket that covers you head to toe, refraining you from enjoying and appreciating reality. It does not matter how exciting or riveting your current activity is, that blanket shields and obstructs your view. But what can you do? For twenty-one days every year you must wait. You must bear the weight of the blanket, and try your best to lift it up and appreciate the current moment. If you don't, you might lose it.

XLV

not lost

"I used to play," you tell them. When was the last time you touched it? Maybe five . . . eight years ago. What was once a daily part of your life has now become extinct. Your schedule is no longer filled with weekly ,and March is no longer the start of the fearful season of festivals. June and August are free for vacations because exams are no longer your worry.

"Yeah, it's hard, balancing school and work," they'll say back. But is it really, though? Was it truly because you were occupied with other priorities that you let the piano go? Or was it because you just didn't want to do it anymore? Maybe it's a bit of both. An awkward silence unravels, and you feel a pulse inside you, wondering if you should have continued with it.

What if you had continued?

The lost artist within you can always be found. That's the beauty of being an artist from the outset. It's never too late and you'll never be too old or wise for the instrument. At the 2019 Royal Conservatory Convocation in Toronto, Honorary Fellow and Olympian Eric Radford said, "An athletic career is limited but a music career can be started at any time." Being an artist is timeless. Being an artist means your canvas is always waiting for you. The piano, though you may not play on it anymore, and though it still sits in the corner untouched after all these years, it will always be there.

The piano you don't play on any more is more than the multi-thousand dollars your parents spent on it. The piano you don't play on any more is more than a symbol of hundreds of missed practice hours, more than a symbol of late night regret and forgotten pieces. The piano you don't play on anymore is home. It will always be your home.

The piano does not ask anything of you, ever. It sits there waiting to be played on, and you must know that its bench is eternally reserved for you. The response that most people give is that they fear they're not good enough; that because they haven't played in years, they won't be as "good" as they used to be; and because they haven't practiced in "so long," what's the point anyway?

Well, in the midst of me preparing for my Elementary Teaching Diploma, I was practicing a level one piece titled "Angelfish." Prior to this, I had been practicing Schumann's Papillons no. 2, a Bach gigue, and one of Haydn's last sonatas. After I finished a run-through of "Angelfish," my dad came down from his upstairs office, he was truly amazed with my performance. It was like nothing he had heard before.

My dad has been around for every practice ever since I started. He has heard every piece from prep level to advanced, and he's very aware of the progress and advancement of my piano studies. Needless to say, he is not a stranger to the complexities of learning the piano and the level that I've worked my way up to.

"Play it again, it sounds like a movie." My first reaction was to laugh. After all these years, and weeks, and days of practicing, my dad had never been moved by any piece I've practiced as much as "Angelfish" at that very moment. On a later thought, I guess it is an elegant piece: both hands begin in the treble clef, where the right hand plays a recurring accompaniment of ascending and descending three-notes. The left hand takes the melody playing the same pitch in different octaves, scattered in between the three-note right hand accompaniment. Every other note, the left hand will cross over the right hand, giving the piece a sense of flare and flexibility. It sounds impressive.

But what I learned the most from my dad's reaction was not that I failed to appreciate the simplicity of a piece or that my first reaction was to chuckle, which reveals poor empathy on my part. Rather, what I learned the most was that levels and grades in music are nothing less than the commercial construct of the music itself. It is that it is actually impossible to draw a line down one piece from the next. That although a piece is labelled "Level One," does not make it any less impressive than a performance level piece. That although a piece is within the elementary level category, does not make it any less beautiful, or elegant, or intricate than a Chopin Nocturne in level nine.

Levels are important because that's how we can metrically measure our progress. We need the levels in piano just as we need grades in school to know where we stand in comparison to everyone else. We need these not to define who we are, but to define where we stand in the realm of our peers so as to foster and cultivate a community.

So if you're feeling like you shouldn't sit at the bench anymore because you're not worthy or because you've let the instrument down by not practicing all these years; know that you do not owe it to anyone to perfect a piece or play something virtuosic. The only thing you owe to your piano is a touch of a note and the warmth you bring when you fill the room with your music. Your music brightens up the world. It need not be complex. It need not be "Angelfish," even.

But you should do it. Take a step towards the corner of your living room. Remove the cloth your mom put over it to prevent dust collection. Open the lid of your bench to reveal old music books or visit the miniature library on the side of your piano. Pull out a piece you remember – it could be as niche or cliché as you wish. Open up the pages and find the key. You'll notice that you haven't forgotten the language of music. You'll notice that you recognize the sharps, and recognize the starting note, and where your left hand follows. You'll notice that your hand will curve itself to the form you need and when you're ready, play.

XLVI

placemaking

We are inhabitants of countries, states and cities. We are tireless participants of human constructed societies with unspoken expected norms and idolized concrete institutions. Our daily lives are built around earning a means to live or pursuing a useful education.

But that is not how we make our place in this world. That is not how we build a home and create a space to find comfort in. That is society's way of placemaking.

We make our place with the way we make our beds (or don't), the way we arrange photo frames by the entrance of the doorway, and the way we stack our books atop the piano in the living room. We make our place with which room we choose to put our plants in, or if we choose to buy fake flowers instead.

Close your eyes. Think about where your piano is placed at home. What kind of piano is it? Is it a digital keyboard that's perpetually plugged into the outlet underneath the window ledge? Is it an old wooden upright that your grandmother passed onto your dad, and the manufacturer's name is rubbed off? Is it a fresh shiny black Yamaha that your mom bought you when you were five because she was determined you'd play until level ten, but it turns out you're still at level seven? Or is it a baby grand with its tail off to the corner, and angled in a way that makes your living room feel like a concert hall that is forever open to listeners?

It does not matter what type of keyboard you have at home, as long as you remember where it is. It does not matter what brand, what kind, what finish, or even if it is in tune. It does not matter that you haven't dusted off the top in a while, or that under the cover of the bench that opens, are the books that you stored away when you were younger.

Try to take in what sits on top of the piano. Is it used as a shelf of décor as many treat it? Is it covered in a white lace table runner with framed pictures of you with Santa Claus from 1996? Or are there piles and piles of sheet music that you printed off a few years ago for Christmas, yet you have not touched ever since?

The place where we make music becomes the universe in which we find ourselves. The place where art comes alive is the same place where we, the artists, catch our breath. The air in that place is invisible, but the sounds that echo from your touch on the keys resonate and wrap around the atmosphere like a velvet cloak.

The place where art comes alive is where sound becomes music, and stillness becomes motion. That although we may be playing and your mom might be in the background speaking to your grandpa; or that your little cousins are running around chasing each other, and almost knocking down the very expensive lamp; or that your dad doing the dishes seems to be drowning out your melody; the velvet cloak is heard. Your music thickens the air and it demands the listeners to feel it; perhaps not with their hands, but with their minds.

Placemaking is important because we are often told that it is the humans that make a place great, or that great company makes for good times. There is truth in this and no doubt it has been proven time and time again. But the careful arrangement of an instrument in a room, coupled with the intricate memory of that arrangement remains sacred. For this is where we have spent our days and nights, practicing away. This is where we have felt our lowest lows and highest highs; where our failures may turn into successes, and successes become legacies. This is where your biggest mistakes were kept safe, and your best runs were never repeated outside the room.

This is your place. This is where you belong, even if it may not feel that way all the time. Being a pianist is challenging, but a virtue on its own. To be given the opportunity to make, learn, and share music is a privilege that only a few of us have the luxury to indulge in. Cherish it.

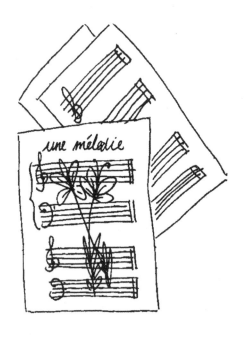

Vignettes of a Pianist

XLVII

the last vignette

The curtain will never close for us. Musicians are musicians until the last song is written or the last note is sung. We will always be behind that fourth wall, serving as the artists and leaders of creation and expression. We serve to create and share the fruits of beauty and what makes us feel "good." There is no last vignette. There will always be vignettes. There will always be moments in life, any life, that are worth remembering, worth talking about, worth reading about. So while most of the time it may feel like we are simply resharing a piece curated from a forefather of Western culture, we are also embodying the next chapter of the human race. We are illustrating the frames and windows of the next set of artists. The next set of humans.

In *La La Land*, there is a quote from my favorite number of the movie-musical:

Here's to the ones who dream

Foolish as they may seem

Here's to the hearts that ache

Here's to the mess we make

We are the fools who dream. We may also be the culprits of heartaches, disappointments, and chaos.

But what is this world without us?

Acknowledgments

The two individuals whom I should inevitably thank and feel the utmost gratitude for are the same two to which this book is dedicated. Mom and Dad I thank you. I thank you for everything you have ever done for me. To say that you have simply given me the gift of music is an understatement. It is not that they have simply given it to me, but fostered it, protected it, and fought for it for me. It is not that they had realized my potential or that they knew it would benefit me for other parts of life, but that they realized the need for one's passion in life and that the word balance is not just about a well-rounded child but a child who brings life full circle. It is bringing me to piano lessons and then hosting recitals of my own under the same roof. It is buying me a piano I both learned and then taught "Mary Had a Little Lamb" on. It is the need to feel the unity and 360 spin around the journey called life and realizing that the greatest lessons in life are found in the belief that we are all destined for greatness. Thank you mom and dad.

The second group I must pay my thanks to is the reason for the publication of this book. First, to Marianne Zin, my colleague and friend who works at The Conservatory of Dance and Music with me. Ky-Lee, head of Golden Brick Road Publishing House, who has guided me and helped me jumpstart my official career as an "author"—a claim I never knew I would be able to make. Then I'd like to thank Lola for giving me such great ideas for illustrations and how to elaborate on each vignette.

I'd also like to thank Cheryl Upper, the Director of the Conservatory of Dance and Music (CDM), where I spend almost half of my life. This space has given me a piece of this life's sanity and joy that I find nowhere else. This place has taught me the importance of community in a workplace and what great things can happen when artists of the same goal—to share their art—come together. Thank you for always believing in me and bringing me on at such a young age. You have given me opportunities to both start and maintain my career that have changed my life completely, to which I am forever grateful.

Next there is a line of teachers and mentors that I will always be grateful for. At the start of my musical journey is Olivia Wong—my very first piano teacher. Though my memory as an aged human does not grant me the vivid recollections of the first series of my piano lessons with you, I know that the abundance of knowledge and the solid foundation you passed onto me has transferred in great strides towards my role as a piano teacher.

I'd also like to thank Sofia Erlichman— who guided me through my years of preteen and teenage angst. You stood by me through my fights with my mom and heartbreaks you never knew of. There must have been lessons where I was awful and you still kept going with me. You taught me the value of practicing and that the only way to move through life is to keep your head high and persevere.

Patricia Lemoine: My hero and my whole life's reason to be in love with my art. Pat, thank you. In the midst of my worst and what felt like pits of a dark cave, you shed light into my passion. You revived my passion. For nine years, we worked together tirelessly and unconditionally. You helped me see the beauty in all art forms and opened my world to new genres in ballet, opera and theatre. You made me realize that hard work does not translate to suffering nor does passion always mean a frozen smile. You taught me that life is about chasing that one thing you love the most—that one element of life that keeps you going. If you find it, you must follow it. You must protect it. Thank you Pat, for all you've done.

In my pedagogical studies, I'd like to thank Mr. James Lawless, whom I had the utmost pleasure of getting to know and study under in 2018-2019. In these years, you helped me grow as a teacher and I've applied your expertise not only through the books and literature you've recommended but also your wise words and insight into the modern teaching world. Your journey inspires me every day.

An individual who most people may not know I have a connection with is Ms. Grace Lin, the founder of Euromusic Centre in Markham, Ontario. This is the place where I took my first piano lesson, bought my first piano, and gave my first performance. Thank you, Ms. Lin, for your words of wisdom, your belief in my passion, and communicating the truths of what it really is like to become an artist—even if those truths are not all pleasant sometimes. I am thankful because your dedication and commitment to the world of the arts is incomparable. Thank you for all you do.

An artist's journey is never accomplished without the inspiration, guidance and support from multiple groups of unconditionally loving and tirelessly working individuals. Thank you to those who have sat through every performance and late night practice session. To all my examiners, adjudicators, judges, teachers, mentors who've provided me with the feedback and honour of your presence to witness and listen to my art, thank you. To my fellow piano colleagues, who I've only crossed paths with during competition festivals and recitals, thank you for sitting through my most embarrassing and triumphant performances; for giving me performance examples to aspire to, and congratulating me when the achievement fell humbly in my hands. To those I have forgotten to mention, or have purposely left out to refrain from leaving anyone out, you will know who you are.

Author

Megan Yim has been teaching piano for over 10 years, and has a diverse academic background in English, French, and Marketing from the University of Toronto and Schulich School of Business in Toronto, Canada. She holds diplomas from the Royal Conservatory of Music in Piano Performance and Piano Pedagogy. *Vignettes of a Pianist* is Megan's first book, which has been a dream for her to combine her passions for music and literature in one composition. Megan started playing piano at age four. She has not stopped playing ever since. When not playing piano, Megan enjoys reading feminist historical fiction, crafting, and planning her next travel itinerary.

GOLDEN BRICK ROAD
PUBLISHING HOUSE

Link arms with us as we pave new paths to a better and more expansive world.

Golden Brick Road Publishing House (GBRPH) is a small, independently initiated boutique press created to provide social-innovation entrepreneurs, experts, and leaders a space in which they can develop their writing skills and content to reach existing audiences as well as new readers.

Serving an ambitious catalogue of books by individual authors, GBRPH also boasts a unique co-author program that capitalizes on the concept of "many hands make light work." GBRPH works with our authors as partners. Thanks to the value, originality, and fresh ideas we provide our readers, GBRPH books are now available in bookstores across North America.

We aim to develop content that effects positive social change while empowering and educating our members to help them strengthen themselves and the services they provide to their clients.

Iconoclastic, ambitious, and set to enable social innovation, GBRPH is helping our writers/partners make cultural change one book at a time.

Inquire today at www.goldenbrickroad.pub